The

Bombshell
BUSINESS WOMAN

The *Bombshell* BUSINESS WOMAN

How to Become a Bold,
Brave, Female Entrepreneur

AMBER HURDLE

Clovercroft Publishing

The Bombshell Business Woman

©2017 by Amber Hurdle

Published by Clovercroft Publishing, Franklin, Tennessee

Published in association with Larry Carpenter of
Christian Book Services, LLC
www.christianbookservices.com

Cover photo by Jessica McIntosh

Edited by Robert Irvin

Copy Edit by Christy Callahan

Cover and Interior Design by Suzanne Lawing

Printed in the United States of America

978-1-945507-47-2

This book is dedicated to my "original Bombshells." You showed up every week, did the work, supported each other, and experienced transformation far beyond business. You confirmed it was merely my job to activate what is already inside professional women worldwide—knowing that women, when confident, will increasingly activate the best in each other.

Foreword

by Pete Weien
General Manager, retired
Gaylord Opryland Resort and Convention Center
Nashville, Tennessee

It was just after the historic 2010 Nashville Flood that I first met Amber as we were actively recruiting a new director of internal communications and events for Gaylord Opryland —a key leadership position and one that would play an even more important role in the months ahead. Just a few weeks before, Opryland was significantly impacted by this unprecedented catastrophe that closed the iconic resort due to more than eight feet of water in the lobby and guest room atriums from the nearby Cumberland River. We had just begun to determine how we could reopen the property in less than two hundred days.

We needed a talented and creative executive who could create a compelling internal public relations strategy to keep the spirits of our three thousand employees high, even though most were temporarily furloughed and without work. Additionally, this individual would have to quickly develop a detailed and far-reaching supporting campaign that would serve as the rallying point to achieve the key business objectives.

After just a few moments of our initial conversation, I knew that we had our director. Amber was charismatic, strong-willed, and exuded a confident "I can absolutely do this" attitude. Little did I know at that time that her faith, early life experiences, and broad business acumen created the sound foundation we needed at such a critical time. Looking back, it was her excellent preparation, deep personal conviction to do the remarkable, and Amber's unwavering support of people that inspired the Opryland team and me to do what most thought could not be accomplished. We needed someone to be "the bomb" and we got a Bombshell Business Woman.

Amber has gone on to assist so many in her consulting practice to better understand the fundamental and necessary principles of business. More importantly, she has helped those who perhaps have become unfocused, possibly as a result of today's information bombardment or other unintended distractions, and which have created personal or professional consequences—often times both.

It is Amber's direct personal engagement and straightforward no nonsense communication approach, as you will see as you read this book, that has lead her to work with a variety of individual entrepreneurs and large organizations.

This book will cause the reader to think, be very intentional and committed to take action, and to do the detailed homework. Follow Amber's comprehensive approach and establish your personal brand, business mojo, and build the right plan that will serve you well, as it has Amber over her life and the many people she has supported.

I hope you will get the chance to met Amber, hear her speak, work with her in person, and become a member of the Bombshell Business Woman nation.

Contents

Acknowledgments

I've been told I'm not content without an incredible challenge before me, so I suppose after completing this book I should be abundantly joyful! Going back to darker seasons to draw on relevant memories was difficult emotionally. Spiritually experiencing God's grace rush over me as I acknowledged how far He's brought me in such a short amount of time was overwhelming. Then, add the technical part of writing, editing, promotional strategy, and more, and this is indeed the furthest I've pushed myself in a long time.

Through this experience, countless people encouraged and uplifted me, for which I'm eternally grateful. While I could write an entire book to acknowledge all of the people who have woven their thread of influence into my life's quilt, ultimately getting me to this moment, I offer the following thanks to those who directly impacted the creation of *The Bombshell Business Woman*.

Geoff, words fail. It takes an incredibly strong man to be my partner. I've never trusted anyone as much as I trust you—to support me when I'm in full-fledged Bombshell mode and when I need to be weak. You've never tried to change me. You are my pillar and I love you with all that is in me. Thank you for having my back through this entire experience.

Thank you, Mom and Dad, for always celebrating individualism, always encouraging me to be 100 percent me, and cheering me on throughout this crazy process. You are my anchor and I love you.

Brittany, Derek, and Kristen: the three of you are the fuel

in my tank, and I love you more than human words can properly express. You've not only been patient as this book consumed so much of my time and emotional energy, you've also been helpful and even conscious of the times I was close to the edge! Thank you for being the best "kids" I could hope for.

Heather, Andrew, Christian, Cameron and Katarina, we are so lucky to have each other as siblings. Thanks for embracing and cheering me on through this and everything that got me here.

Angiee Korman and Mark Lee, thank you for your longstanding, trustworthy, and consistent friendships in all circumstances. Through all of my crazy ideas, my victories and defeats, and through the many evolutions of Amber, you've been there. My heart is full of your love deposits. I adore you.

Austin Netzley, your friendship is treasured on so many levels, yet this book was concretely formed because of your pushing, encouragement, and help. Thank you.

Michelle Moore, we always say, "Iron sharpens iron." I think you've been sharpening at warp speed! Thanks for the shove to prioritize and finalize this book, and for walking alongside me as a trusted friend on this journey.

Pete Weien, I told you I would never let you off the hook when it comes to pushing me to be better, and I think I've proven it! Thank you for being a source of encouragement, critical thinking, and even a lifeline when I need one. Our "Peteings" have always been a catalyst for greatness, and I hope you see the impact of your influence in this book.

Larry Carpenter, my publisher aka the conductor of my book orchestra, this would not have happened without you. Thank you for your wisdom, straight talk, and speed. God brought me you on a silver platter and I'm grateful. Likewise, Bob Irvin, my content editor, thank you for going in with the hazmat suit, and ruthlessly editing while allowing all of my

Amberisms and . . . errr . . . spunk to remain. The content editing might have been the most fun and the easiest part thanks to you! Christy Callahan, thank you for your eagle eye and for batting cleanup in the copyediting stage. The perfectionist in me bows to the perfectionist in you. Suzanne Lawing, thank you for designing a gorgeous book. This team is incredible.

Thank you to Scott Sears and Will Weisiger at Flyte Old World Dining for allowing me to capture the cover photo in a special place to me and so many others. Jessica McIntosh, thank you for being the best photographer in the universe (and my friend) and for getting the money shot for this cover.

Dr. Gary Gallant, you've been putting Humpty Dumpty back together again for years and years, but the past several months have had its own health challenges as I've really pushed the boundaries of my baseline chronic condition: "overdoing-it-itis." I don't know how people get through life without a doctor and friend like you. Thank you for being you and giving me space to be me at my most authentic.

Last, but not least, thank you to my peeps! God bless my L-Town tribe for the never-ending support and love! Cheers to '80s/'90s dance parties, weekly hot wing binges, group text abuse, random gifts and visits when my energy is noticeably low, and to absurdly intense daily workouts completed in the name of sanity! Of course, also thank you to X Mastermind for being my safe place and my go-to for resources and professional help from the beginning, but specifically as I've developed this book. My friends have always been an extraordinary source of strength and energy. Y'all rock my face off!

What *Is* a Bombshell?

When you think about the term *bombshell*, you might think of a gorgeous woman who enters a room and instantly commands attention from everyone around her. But is this because she is strikingly beautiful? Or is it because she is overtly confident in herself, walking in with a refreshing, attention-getting boldness?

I say the latter.

That's why, after years of working with women who are what I call next-level talented, yet still too often succumbing to measuring their worth on the few weaknesses they had, I have redefined the term.

I started calling my female professional clients Bombshells so I could routinely speak truth into their lives, reminding them of all they were created to do and all they had, and were, accomplishing as driven professional women. (Friendly disclaimer: Throughout this book, you'll see me capitalize *Bombshell* because the term, as I define it, is that important. Being the rule breaker I am, I want to draw attention to how amazingly special you are as a *Bombshell*; you're not just a bombshell. So yes, I'm aware the dictionary would say to lowercase the term. But yes, it's that important to me. And yes, I had to talk my editor into it!)

THE WAY OF THE BOMBSHELL

According to my definition, a Bombshell, at her best, is a bold, brave, and unwaveringly confident woman in business and in life.

Her talents are remarkable, and she knows how to direct them to create change in the lives of others. She is not just driven. She is *called.*

A Bombshell cannot be satisfied without her work being a significant part of her life. If she is a mother, she loves her children more than life. In fact, she knows this is her greatest role, yet she is almost embarrassed to admit out loud that it is not who she is entirely.

A Bombshell's identity rests in her professional work because that's where she sees consistent, positive results. It's where she wins. No matter how messy it gets, she can figure out the path to excellence. When her gifts and talents manifest in that setting and she's on a winning streak, she feels more equipped to lead and navigate her personal life.

What's more, the thought of being a stay-at-home mom is not appealing to a Bombshell. She looks at her friends who are gifted in keeping their homes, raising their children as their primary focus, and making Pinterest-perfect teacher gifts at Christmas, and she sometimes wonders: *What's wrong with me?*

When she's tired and left to overthink, a Bombshell wonders if she is missing out, if she's not being a "good enough" mom or wife.

In fact, many Bombshells are or have been the primary providers in their homes, but even those who can choose not to work outside the home find themselves unfulfilled and bored without a career to flex their intellectual muscles.

Then, while little Susie's mom brings cupcakes decorated in the school colors and mascot while elegantly sitting on a three-tiered stand dripping in crystals, a Bombshell's children sign up for the paper plates for class parties.

Every time.

This is where, despite all her amazing gifts, no matter all her professional accomplishments, and even aware of how well-rounded her children actually are, a Bombshell loses her confidence. Over a package of paper plates!

(It clearly takes extra human strength and intelligence to be a stay-at-home mom, by the way. It is just not the path that makes a Bombshell come alive. To be clear: every woman has her path, and it takes all women fulfilling their callings to make the world go round.)

A Bombshell who is a single woman, on the other hand, is forever annoyed that instead of being asked about her business or countless successes, she is most often asked if she is "seeing someone," ever "going to settle down," or if she "plans to have children."

The thing is, she is more focused on creating the best, most independent version of herself so that if she does, in fact, want to one day enter a committed relationship, she knows she is a whole person uniting with a partner who will complement, not complicate, her life. She travels and eats well. She creates her own agenda and priorities, and can't for the life of her figure out why everyone around her is so obsessed with weddings and babies.

Never mind the fact that many of her friends have been married and divorced all before she's gotten around to becoming engaged once. Yet even she, when left alone to think too much about that last wedding invitation received in the mail, second-guesses herself.

Over one more wedding invitation!

In fairness, it's easier than ever for today's professional woman to succumb to these temporary insecurity traps because now they exist in a social media-edited world. They must be smart but not too smart; beautiful but not too sexy; savvy but not perceived as manipulative; empathetic but not too emotional; strong but not too masculine; equipped as a leader but not too dominant. And the list goes on of what they *should* be or how they *should* act or what they *should* do.

No matter what they do, there is always someone "shoulding" on them, so in these private moments of weakness, it is easier to create the voice in her own mind to simply beat everyone to the punch. That way, she doesn't have to feel defeated and marginalized . . . again.

So a Bombshell's constant struggle is living up to her God-given potential while also battling in her mind the difference between her expectations and the world's expectations.

A Bombshell wants it all, yet she is beginning to see she can't have it all at once.

She cherishes her family. She embraces community. She has a heart to volunteer and lead, even outside of her business. Yet, she is likely a recovering workaholic, a woman who has already dealt with the relational, physical, and emotional consequences of an unbalanced life.

That's a major reason she made the scary leap to entrepreneurship—so she can have more time freedom and live life on her own terms. Her business exists so she can share her greatest gifts with her customers while also being present as a wife, mother, daughter, friend, and more.

Because nonstop work without an amazing personal life is not what she wants either.

So the concept of "work-life balance" is a fleeting idea for a Bombshell. Instead, a focus on work-life *success*—where her time and energy shifts based on the rotating demands of each area of her life—is far more realistic.

That's when a Bombshell at her best stands proud in who she is and what she offers the world, and when she can abandon the whirlwind of uncertainty.

She embraces a *fearless*, unapologetic expectation of being compensated for sharing her gifts and knowledge by understanding her profit center and the results she delivers.

A *Bombshell commands attention* for her business with a strong culture, consistent branding, and simple, no-to-low-cost marketing.

She creates amazing word-of-mouth marketing because she attracts the right clients, who fall in love with her brand experience thanks to her solid structure and business processes.

And when she does these things, her business does not run her; she instead runs her business. She is then freed up to fully embrace her personal life and live more abundantly in all areas.

Do these desires, struggles, and realizations sound familiar? Then you must be a Bombshell!

Not feeling too much like a full-fledged Bombshell as you picked up this book? Then let me bestow upon you the official title of a Bombshell. Own it. Claim it. *Work it.* Then go through the steps I'll provide in this book to become one.

BECOMING A BOMBSHELL WOMAN

You know you have it in you, but sometimes the overwhelming feeling becomes too much and you find yourself back on the hamster wheel. Whether you want to take things to the next level or you're just getting started, this book could be your ticket to freedom—freedom from wasting time, energy, and money on your business and getting dismal results.

You want to do it "the right way," but you're not even sure what that looks like! Who do you compare yourself to when you are pacing harder and faster than everyone you are looking to?

I see you, Sister. You are working your bootie off, trying to become the go-to business in your industry, to create an amazing place to work for your employees, and ultimately to do it all in less time while making more money so you can actually enjoy your personal life.

Creating a plan that works for your *unique* business in your *unique* market for your *unique* customers might just be the one thing you've been looking for so you can finally start getting the business traction you want.

Unfortunately, planning is the least sexy part of entrepreneurship. Nobody is liking or retweeting your plan, so there's no instant reward.

The good news is, planning is my jam.

I've created hundreds and hundreds of communication plans and events across my career, so my mind automatically operates in that way. Honestly, my current consulting business started out working exclusively with corporate clients. I was focused on hard-core executive coaching, senior leadership strategic planning, and leadership training for middle managers.

Then I started getting female business owners, who were *super* talented, coming to me asking for help with clear direction and solid plans. I saw them caught in an unnecessary whirlwind. So I started simplifying big branding and marketing concepts that I learned from my public relations degree and marketing minor, as well as my career experience, and began implementing them, putting them into easy-to-digest, easy-to-implement steps for the average business owner. This is the woman who is really good at her craft, but perhaps struggles with the business side of things.

Now, I'm going to help you.

By the time you finish this book and download the free online resources available on my website, www.thebombshellbusinesswoman.com, you will have solid brand standards and a marketing plan, efficient business systems, and a strategic way to actually run your business so your business doesn't run you—and you will have established exactly what you want from your business and life. You'll begin reeling in the work and life success you want.

Wait. Are those the hallelujah angels singing?

But here's maybe the best part: Once you have all this worked out, you can implement this plan yourself or hand it off to someone on your team or hire someone to implement it for you. Since they'll have a road map designed by *you*, you know they'll do it the right way—your way. Not that I'm calling you a control freak. (Who am I kidding? Yes, I am.)

There's no need to stay up all night or take hours away from your operation and urgent demands trying to figure this out. In fact, it's time for you to take the pressure off and stop trying to earn your marketing degree at the same time you are busy rocking hair behind the chair, providing legal counsel, selling a home, or whatever it is you do best. Instead, you need to create a solid foundation that all decisions, marketing or otherwise, can be based on.

The plans you will create throughout *The Bombshell Business Woman* will give you a step-by-step guide, showing you exactly how to make your business irresistible.

Once you've designed your plan for your unique business, you've done the heavy lifting for good. From there, you can tweak the essentials as your business evolves and grows. Once you build the foundation, everything else starts to fall into place.

WHAT TO EXPECT FROM *THE BOMBSHELL BUSINESS WOMAN*

There will be no fluff.

While unicorns are awesome, none were harmed—nor

even called upon—in the making of this book. Nor fairies, for that matter. Nope, we're not going there.

So you don't have to worry about any woo-woo stuff coming out in the midst of plainly spoken actionable advice. I will teach theory you can actually put into practice.

I will use what I call my velvet machete, meaning I'm going to shoot you straight, but I'm going to do it because I care that much about your success.

You'll be encouraged and uplifted. I believe in you so much I wrote an entire stinking book to support you! (Which, as it turns out, is as hard as everyone says it is!)

I will never ask you to follow a business trend or fad. I will teach you both old school and new-fashioned ways of running your business, and I will challenge you to identify if it's a fit for *your* unique business. Because I'm all about personalization. No one knows what is going to work for you but you.

Throughout this book, you will have to make tough decisions to properly align your business with your purpose. Just get ready for it. It's going to be OK. If you can embrace delayed gratification, the end result of ongoing decision-making will be extraordinary.

Becoming a thriving Bombshell is on the other side of your comfort zone. But you, Sister, have it in you. So if you want to become a bold, brave, unwaveringly confident fempreneur (female entrepreneur), keep reading. I encourage you to read the book through once, then go back to each chapter to complete the suggested Take Action Bombshell exercises or download the exercises, along with the other free online resources, at thebombshellbusinesswoman.com.

Cheers to embarking on your Bombshell adventure!

One

Made in God's Image

Before we dive into tactical ways to conquer the battles of a Bombshell Business Woman, it's important to address your beliefs at a gut level. As someone who received her PhD through the School of Hard Knocks, I know that the empowerment side of things is equally important as any business lesson. After all, if you don't have the right mind-set, your headspace will be overcrowded with counterproductive thinking instead of clarity and intention.

Plus, if you don't believe you can do something, how are you going to get your employees, an investor, your business partner, or a customer to believe you can do it? If you can't sell yourself on your abilities, how are you going to sell everyone else?

The bottom line is, if you don't expect more, you won't get more. So it's time to set some expectations of what you want of yourself and from life.

"Well, Amber, that's easier said than done," you might be saying.

Maybe you're wondering how I can be so stinkin' confident. I joke that there was a complication at birth and my give-a-durn busted, but the truth is, I was taught well.

While I'd be lying if I said I didn't have my own set of insecurities and limiting beliefs, I can say that from very early on I simply made a decision to be grateful for how God chose to make me.

You see, I read in the Bible, from a very young age, that I was made in God's image.

In *God's image*!

I mean, let those words hit you over the head. Who am I to argue with the Creator of the universe? Who am I to say that I am not a masterpiece?

And beyond that, with billions of people in the world, why would I fret over a small handful of people who don't see me in that light?

REDHEADED, FAIR-SKINNED, AND FRECKLED

When I was born, it was clear that my Scottish roots kicked my Italian and Norwegian genes in the pants.

I have always been redheaded, fair-skinned, and freckled. In a word: different.

While I've observed plenty of other redheads getting teased, I honestly can only recount one instance when someone—a boy in my fourth-grade class—made a snarky comment to me. He merely called me Carrot Top, to which I quickly replied, "Carrot tops are green, you idiot."

I probably rolled my eyes, and then went on about my little fourth-grade business.

No one ever came at me with a stupid redhead joke again.

I wasn't slowing down to wallow in what was clearly a small-minded comment with no purpose other than an attempt to make this boy look cool.

Too bad for him it backfired.

The reality is, I rather enjoyed being different from everyone else. It made me unique.

It made me special. *God* made me special.

So, I have a question for you: *Do you believe that about yourself?*

My early ability to embrace me just as I was created began by first honoring my physical characteristics, ones that very few around me shared.

So now I ask you: Don't you also have unique attributes, whether physical or intrinsic (like values, strengths, or talents), that you can also start honoring?

What do you know about yourself that you aren't boldly sharing? I challenge you to brainstorm a list of at least five things now!

BUILT ON A STRONG FOUNDATION

Perhaps standing tall in who I was made to be was a bit deep for a little girl to understand, but I was raised by a redheaded mother who was teased incessantly as a child. I supposed this gave her a lifetime to consider how to build up her own child and encourage her to embrace her uniqueness.

What's more, my father is a world-class drummer who literally walks to the beat of his own drum. Not to mention, I was routinely around his musician friends who, frankly, didn't need anyone's approval to rock. My dad modeled, through example, how to do the relationship thing without having a need to conform or try to fit in.

Diversity, on so many levels, is celebrated in my family. That strong foundation enabled me to view each stage of life through a lens of appreciation first.

I understand not every adult had the same type of childhood I did, and the foundations of others may be far shakier. Yet now is the time to start demolishing the lies that no longer serve you. It's time to dig through the rubble until you can pull out only the truths of who you are and why you matter in this world.

I'm speaking to those of you who have made bad decisions in your past. I'm speaking to those of you who feel like you've never really recovered from being hurt by somebody. Whether someone let you down, abandoned you, or just plain ol' broke your heart—or if you managed to hurt yourself all on your own—things get uncertain when the past comes to haunt us.

The truth is, no matter what's happened in your past, no matter who's let you down, no matter what type of shame you feel for the decisions you've made, there is a future ahead of you, and it's a clean slate. There is always the next step and there is always, always, *always* hope.

I have the privilege of hindsight thanks to the plethora of poor decisions I've made in my life. Now I use those data points and lessons learned in a constructive way to carefully map out my life and, importantly, to speak truth into other people's lives.

Any wisdom I offer comes from loads of life experience. My friend Mark, one of two friends who know the darkest parts of me and love me still, likes to say that you can't measure a person by model year; you have to measure that person by their mileage. And that's the truth.

I've had women in my office who are stuck and don't know why. We're talking about business: strategic planning, branding, employee issues, and the like, and I can sense with every bit of me that something is festering at a very deep level.

So I ask point-blank: "What's really going on? What's really holding you back? Where is this resistance coming from?"

Inevitably, there is some story my client is telling herself on repeat that is so loud she can't focus on the steps she needs to next-level her efforts.

I have cried in my office with women who are just so burdened by yesterday that they can't even begin to think about tomorrow. And it doesn't matter how strong or accomplished the woman is, the lies have grabbed her by the ovaries and won't let go.

But the gift I get to unpack time and again these days is looking women in the eyes and telling them about my own journey. I can show just how far from grace I fell, and what it took to first claw my way out of desperation and then to grow personally and professionally far more than I thought possible.

I find myself saying to clients, "You hired me to elevate your brand and your clientele. But I can't take you to the next level if I'm digging you out of a ditch."

So before we talk about how to next-level your business and life, let me tell you about the ditch I dug for myself—and then promptly plunged into.

Two

Sixteen and Pregnant

When I was in high school, my family moved from Orange County, California, to a rural area of Middle Tennessee; it was quite the adjustment. Talk about a culture shock: going from everything being open 24/7, lots of malls and shopping, and ample stuff to do. (I mean, I could literally sit on my roof and watch the Disneyland fireworks during the summer.) Suddenly, I was living in a small city that was excited about its second McDonald's!

As if that was not enough to throw a teenager into bona fide '90s *My So-Called Life*-level angst, I also came face-to-face, for the first time, with blatant, daily racism. I came from a private school with many different types of people. Lots of different types of backgrounds, ethnicities, cultures, and experiences. It was really a beautiful thing that not everybody looked like each other. I had Vietnamese friends and Korean friends. I had a friend from Guatemala, a friend from Brazil, and friends from India, Mexico, and many places in the world. How in the world did I end up in a city that had a race riot the year before?

That did a number on me. I simply didn't understand.

The beautiful thing that came from that race riot is that civic leaders, or, really, community leaders—just people like moms and dads—came together and said, "This isn't good enough for our community." They also brought into the discussion those of us at the school who expressed leadership characteristics.

When I moved there I was like, *Well, if I'm going to be here, I may as well dive on in.* So I got involved with all the different school clubs and extracurricular activities and just dove in headfirst. I was asked to help start a group called All Races Together. My leadership in this little group actually garnered some extra attention. Because of my involvement in its leadership and in Students Taking A Right Stand (STARS), I was nominated by someone in our district when Nashville's Channel 4 News reached out and said, "Hey, who are the really great kids in your school district?"

I was selected along with a small handful of other kids in the Middle Tennessee area. We were the "good kids." All they were doing was basically highlighting our involvement, what a good high school kid does and looks like. That was it; that was completely the reason for them following us around. I'm not patting myself on the back here. In fact, I'm just laying the foundation for the fall.

The news cameras followed me around school and were there when we all went to downtown Nashville for a group interview.

When they came to my school one day, we were in this quad-type area outside, and they were asking me a bunch of questions. One of the questions had the word *everyone* in it.

Now, my parents taught me that you don't use the words *everyone, everything, always, never,* and *no one.* Those are strong words, and unless you genuinely mean that *everyone*—as in every single person in the world—should be included in your statement, then don't use the word.

Well, the interviewer said, "So, parents are really concerned, and they think that everyone in high school is having sex. Is that true?" With my small knowledge and my understanding of what it meant to say words like *everyone, everything,* and *all the time,* I answered, "No, not everyone's having sex."

That's the truth. I can guarantee that not every single high schooler in all of the world in 1995 and 1996 was having sex! Further, they did not ask me if I was. But luckily for me—ahem—that was the little sound-bite they selected.

Suddenly, the TV announcer would say, "Check out all these great kids. These high schoolers who are doing great things. Tonight at six and ten!" Then, cut to Amber saying, "No, not everybody's having sex" in my fresh-out-of-Cali Valley girl accent.

Capture that snapshot before I tell you what happens next. Remember, I'm involved in all these different school groups, so much so that I'm on Channel 4 News. Then, "Not everyone is having sex" is the sound-bite that's going out twice a day, every single day, for five days in a row.

PREGNANT AT SIXTEEN

Suddenly, I started feeling not so well in the mornings. I even would tell my mom, "Gosh, I've been getting a lot of headaches lately." Or, "You know, I don't think that grapefruit juice is sitting well with me. I kind of spit that up this morning."

Now, none of that should've been much cause for concern. I'd had digestive issues, even been hospitalized for them, since I was a very small child. As individual events, none of these things seemed like a big deal.

Then one day, my mom's friend brought her a book she had borrowed: *What to Expect If You're Expecting*. If you've ever had a baby, I'm sure you've heard of it.

I did not pick up that book because I thought I might be pregnant. That was the furthest thing from my mind! I picked up the book because it was next to me and I'm a reader, so I started thumbing through it.

I get to the "How Do You Know If You're Pregnant?" section. I'm just reading along for giggles as my mom sits on the couch next to me.

I recall it explaining that when your hormones shift, it causes headaches, and then you start to feel queasy in the morning and foods that normally sit right with you no longer do. You tend to get achy and you're tired a lot.

As I read these things, I had this sudden realization: *I'm pregnant*. I just knew. It listed every single weird thing that I'd been experiencing that I guess I just never put together because I was too busy being a high school student, doing all the leadership things, and being featured on Channel 4 News! I was too busy to notice the fact that I had all the symptoms of pregnancy. My mom's sitting right there. I'm just like, *Oh, my gosh*.

Of course, scared out of my mind, I took a pregnancy test. As soon as I took the test—bam! Two lines. No question. I was pregnant. I went to a clinic. Bam! Two lines again. For sure, I was pregnant.

Now, obviously, there are all kinds of things that go through your mind when you're sixteen years old and find out you're pregnant. From, *How's this going to work?* to, *How am I going to go to college?* to, yes, *How am I going to pay for this kid?*

I mean, I found out I was having a baby before I was even qualified to take the SAT or the ACT.

I even considered what adoption would look like, what

abortion would look like, and if I should try to hide it from my parents. There was a series of emotions, questions, and feelings that consumed me as I knew that, no matter what, my life would change forever.

I decided I could not personally live with any other decision than to step up to the new life I had created for myself. To be clear, that was the right decision for me, and I withhold judgment toward anyone who makes different decisions. My energy stays plenty occupied trying to remove the plank from my own eye, so there's not much left to try to get the speck out of other people's eyes.

For me, there was nothing so scary in my newly discovered future that I could not love my child through.

Little did I know exactly how scary it would get.

In a nanosecond, I went from a very involved leader in my high school and church to suddenly saying, "OK, now I'm going to be a mom."

This was the shift that forever changed my life.

FACING MY PARENTS

Of course, I had to tell my parents.

Coincidentally, just a few weeks before I discovered I was pregnant, my mom and I were watching the *Sally Jessy Raphael* talk show. (Now, I know all you youngins won't know who that is, but back in the day, before reality TV, we had afternoon talk shows. Sally Jesse was one of the most popular.)

In this episode, the guests were teenage girls who were telling their moms they were pregnant. (Because, obviously, national television is the best place to do that.) Anyway, I just remember telling my mom, "Wow, I would never be able to look you in the face and tell you I was pregnant. Oh my gosh! I don't know how they're doing that."

My mom just looked at me and said, "Don't ever say that."

Now, pause. Time-out. My mom was the strict one. My mom was the one you feared. My mom is a loving woman, and being a mom has always been her number one priority, even though she was a career woman who also worked her tail off. But I repeat: my mom was the strict one. OK, on with the story.

She continued: "Don't ever say that. There's nothing that you could ever do that would make me stop loving you. I might not agree with the decision that you make, but I will always, always love you and stick with you."

I remember thinking, *Huh. OK. That's cool.* You know? Like: what a solid mom. As an overachiever who had to have straight As while being the best at everything I tried, I knew in that moment that even if I screwed up, my mom (and dad) would love me through it.

Fast-forward to the night when I finally got the gumption to tell my mom what was going on. As a daddy's girl, I waited until my dad went to sleep because I needed to focus on one angsty conversation at a time, and the mom conversation was the one I needed to conquer first. That was due to a combination of reverent fear and knowing I would need to borrow her extraordinary strength from that point on to endure being covered in shame.

I don't even remember the words I used. I just told her what was going on.

In one sentence, she said everything I needed to know it was going to be OK. "I'm disappointed in the decisions you've made, but there is nothing negative or bad about a baby. A baby is always a blessing."

I began to sob. I was still scared out of my mind about the big picture, but my mom was in agreement with me that my baby was a gift and not a burden.

She had some questions, of course, and we talked about realities like my health, school, and basic lifestyle changes. Then she said it. "OK. We've got to wake up your dad."

In my mind, it was kind of like in a movie when someone is running toward a disaster in slow motion, and inside you're screaming, *Noooooooooooooooooo!*

"Let's just wait until the morning!" I answered (unconvincingly, I guess). "We should let him sleep. You know, it's late."

"No, it is totally unfair that I know and your dad doesn't know," she insisted. "We need to tell your dad."

Dying a thousand deaths inside, I geared up mentally to have the worst conversation ever, part two.

I knew my dad would love me through anything, because he had always been open about all the mistakes he made while living a musician's life. Not to mention I watched him show love and grace to the unlovable and imperfect my entire life. I just couldn't stand to disappoint him.

My dad came out to the family room from a cold sleep. I mean, when sheep can't sleep, they count my dad. Watching him trying to focus on me and what I needed so late in the night, I quietly broke down and told him what I had done.

His first question was, "Are you going to finish school?"

"Yes, sir, certainly will," I said. "I promise."

"Finish school," he instructed, half-awake and squinting his eyes. "We'll figure it out. Your education is your future and this baby's future. I love you."

I want to make clear how privileged I am. I understand having supportive parents who loved me through all of this is something not everybody gets. I know people get kicked out of their homes, or maybe they get to live in their homes, but they're chastised.

Neither of my parents ever, ever, *ever* said, "Well, if you wouldn't have gotten pregnant," or, "Well, we're not the ones who got pregnant," or, "These are just the consequences of the decision of you having a baby when you're a teenager."

Once we all knew I was going to be a teen mom, we simply accepted what was and moved on, focusing on the positivity of a new life.

A MATTER OF LIFE OR DEATH

Fast-forward through the terrible pregnancy, which was especially difficult for a teenager who did not understand at the time that I have multiple autoimmune issues . . . to the day Brittany was born.

She came in the middle of a hot July night. I woke up thinking, *I finally did it. I've had that moment in pregnancy. I peed on myself.*

So I got up, made it to the threshold of my door en route to the restroom, and it happened. My water broke.

It was go time.

Oh. My. Gosh. I was about to go into labor.

Terrified at the prospect of pushing a watermelon-sized baby through a golf ball-sized hole, I vomited until I could barely breathe. Then, there I sat, hugging the toilet, my belly pressed up against the cold porcelain, crying useless tears that would not change one thing about what was about to go down.

I collected myself, set my mind to be as strong as my parents had always been for me, then proceeded to wake up everyone who was home that night.

To my relief, my best friend's mom was one of the nurses on duty, and she immediately took over my care. She called her house right away to let my friend know I was in labor.

Barefoot, he rode his brother's bike to the hospital in the middle of the night so he could be the first person there.

I'll bet your best friend didn't recall that memory when

signing your high school yearbook.

The waiting room slowly filled with family, friends, church members, and more. It was a full house.

Lying in a hospital room, feet jacked up in the air with strangers coming and going . . . well, suffice it to say this certainly got me over my medical modesty.

It was surreal.

Yet even as I labored, that spitfire inside of me came out from the depths of my soul. Perfectly aware that I had just started adulthood behind the eight ball, I made a promise to my daughter that day.

This child is going to have every single opportunity that any other child would have who was not born to a teen mom.

At the age where I was supposed to be thinking about my college education, I told myself then that when Brittany reached my age, I was going to be certain she could go to whatever college she wanted and become whomever she wanted.

It was one part scrappy redhead saying, "I'll show you" to the world, and three parts boundless love for this child who did not ask to be born into these circumstances.

That promise became my big why, and that day is deeply etched into my soul.

I had several hours to think about the changes that were about to occur in my life, and then the physical pain took over my attention. After seventeen and one half hours of labor, I wanted more epidural.

Unfortunately, a nurse explained, "If we give you any more, you won't be able to feel to push."

My daughter's head crowned; we were in full-throttle labor. Telling me I could not have more epidural was not what I wanted to hear.

I began pushing. It was as awful as I imagined it would be and then some. Seriously, who voluntarily signs up for this?

Suddenly, my doctor says, "Uh-oh."

Quickly turning to her, my mom asks, "What's uh-oh?"

"Uh-oh," my doctor repeated.

I do not remember a lot from that very stressful day, but I distinctly remember the doctor saying that little phrase twice.

A tsunami-level combination of panic and indignation set in.

My mom promptly insisted, "No matter what is going on, you need to tell Amber. She does better when she knows the truth." And the good Lord knows, that is true to this day.

She explained that my daughter had the umbilical cord wrapped around her neck twice. Essentially, every time I pushed, I choked her.

My baby's heart rate was dropping rapidly, my vitals revealed I was in jeopardy, and the whole situation was quickly spinning out of control.

Before I could process what was happening, I was wheeled into a surgical room and a hard, clear plastic mask was strapped over my nose and mouth.

"Count backward from ten," a serious voice commanded.

I remember saying, "Ten." I don't remember making it to nine.

According to my surgical reports (and my scar) my doctor literally ripped me open to get Brittany out in record time. I know that is graphic, but I want you to understand. Sixteen years old, girl. I was sixteen. Years. Old. I want you to understand the trauma of what was going on.

Come to find out, between me saying the word *ten* and barely getting to say, "Hello, welcome to the world," they took Brittany out of me under extremely stressful conditions. The pediatrician on call carried Brittany out of the surgical room and into a room to revive her. En route, her little leg flopped out from underneath the receiving blanket and it was "Smurf blue," according to several people.

It was later recounted to me that everyone just assumed he was taking her somewhere where I could say my final good-byes once I woke up. Apparently, the dozens of people in the waiting room thought this was the end. My mom passed out at the sight of her little limp limb, and everyone who was waiting on this baby to be born suddenly turned their thoughts to supporting me through my grief.

I wish I could explain exactly what happened in that room that saved my daughter, but all I know is that she was alive—yet still not out of the woods.

When I woke up, I remember they brought Brittany to me in a clear cart with small holes in the side that you could barely reach your hand through. Still groggy from my anesthesia, I touched my newborn's hand for less than three minutes through one of those small holes.

Then they sent her off in the "Angel Mobile," an emergency vehicle used to transport babies to Vanderbilt University Medical Center's neonatal intensive care unit, which was about thirty miles west of where I gave birth. She had to get to a trauma hospital and fast.

As it turns out, Brittany lost a lot of oxygen and swallowed a lot of blood. There were actually all kinds of things that went wrong, but they took her to the best place in the region for her to receive care. Meanwhile, I was in the hospital for nearly three full days trying to recover from my own surgery. I called the NICU every couple of hours to ask about the daughter I had barely met. The nurses indulged me and encouraged me to call as many times as I wished.

Once released from the hospital, I drove back and forth to see Brittany during visiting hours. The first time I held my baby, she had an IV stuck in her scalp because she was such a fighter, so feisty. She would take the IV out of her arm, or her leg, or wherever they had taped it down. They literally had to sedate her and stick it in her head so she couldn't get to it.

To recap, I went through seventeen and a half hours of labor, felt every bit of it, was rushed into an emergency C-section, was told that everyone thought my baby had died, then didn't get to see my kid for three days. Then, when given an opportunity to finally hold her, there is an IV stuck in her scalp. Oh, and I was nonstop pumping and freezing breast milk so she could still get the most nutrition possible while also trying to learn how to breastfeed a baby who went three days without her mother, and all this while recovering from major surgery. At sixteen.

I don't even know how to explain where I was emotionally at that point. I'm a strong person today, and I was a strong person then. However, this was overwhelming physically, mentally, and emotionally. The only glue that held me together was my faith.

The day I got to bring her home, about two weeks later, the doctors repeatedly warned, "Brittany lost a lot of oxygen, so she might be a little slow. Be patient with her development." And there was a list of other disclaimers. Notably among them, they told me that since she had a blood transfusion, she would need to have regular HIV tests for a period of her childhood.

Imagine taking all that in. I was a kid being given responsibility for a kid who needed ongoing HIV testing.

Yet, despite—or perhaps *because of*—this overwhelming feeling, I felt compelled to tell the doctors, "My daughter's a fighter. She's going to be fine."

The fact she had to be sedated and restrained to keep her from removing her IV told me that. Her active gaze and attentiveness showed me she was going to be OK.

Later recognized in the top 10 percent of her high school

class, Brittany was, in fact, a quick learner. She walked for the first time at seven months, talked in full sentences very early, and was always ahead of the development curve. None of the doctors' well-intentioned warnings ended up being true. Still, at sixteen years old or thirty, such statements by doctors about one's child are especially ominous.

But what a thirty-year-old worries about upon returning home from the hospital and what a sixteen-year-old worries about are different.

Delighted that I was in a routine at home with my daughter, I just knew I could successfully nurse her so she could be healthy. The problem was she had extreme reflux, so every time I fed her, she projectile-vomited all over me. Since she had to eat so much because she couldn't keep anything down, I developed mastitis and had to stop nursing. As if that wasn't enough, she didn't really sleep through the night because she spent the first two weeks of her life being poked and prodded every couple of hours to evaluate her medical state.

This whole time, I'm trying to process becoming a mother, process the fact that my baby almost died, that it seemed as if everybody else in the universe got to hold my child before I did, and that she had electrodes stuck to her chest and a needle coming from her head when I finally got the chance. Then, I get her home and I can't even feed her the way I thought would be most nourishing. Finally, I was getting no sleep.

Meanwhile, I'm a mere three weeks away from starting a new high school year.

Picking out my backpack for the year wasn't exactly my priority when I was busy packing a diaper bag.

But I sucked it up, finished school, and we lived happily ever after.

Just kidding.

Seriously, it got worse. It got so much worse.

If you think the decisions that led me to become a teen mom were my greatest moments of foolishness, I assure you I was just warming up.

Even with loving parents who had a strong faith in God, I still had to face the circumstances of a traumatic birth experience, the pressures of being a kid raising a kid, and all the relational issues I won't even get into because it would be a one-sided story. All of this sent me into a lengthy depression.

Now. To address the obvious question you are thinking at this point: there was a father in the picture. Very much in the picture at that time, and very much in agreement with me that our daughter's life was more important than whatever we had going on in high school. We were in a situation that was almost destined to fail, and fail at our relationship we most assuredly did. As adults, we asked each other for forgiveness for how we hurt each other when we were young and overwhelmed. Beyond that, no matter what, I chose to be grateful that he was part of my daughter being a part of my life.

Yet at the time I was hurt. Everything I hoped for my future and the future of my daughter was no longer in plain view.

Like any teenager, I rebelled, and I set the pattern that I adhered to for far too many years after this season of life: I didn't want to hurt anyone else with my stupidity, but I was just fine hurting myself. Because, I would tell myself, *If I was just stronger, I could handle it all. If I was smart enough, I could figure it out.*

Yet since I couldn't, in reality, do those things, I found ways to gut-punch myself every chance I got.

I lost that feisty little redheaded, that freckled girl inside of me who knew she was made in God's image.

I was out of fight. Out of energy. Hope was hanging by a thread.

Three

Life Lessons from the Teen Mom Trenches

At the height of my financial struggle, when I was about nineteen, I had four jobs. There were multiple months where I came home two nights out of every week and didn't sleep at all. *At all.* I went from job to job to job, came home, took a shower, fed my daughter breakfast, and then took her to an educational preschool. It cost way more money than I could afford, but my daughter was super smart, and I refused to leave her somewhere where she just watched Barney all day, every day. I needed her to actually use that incredible brain of hers that the doctors warned might be slow to develop.

I remember one time when I fell asleep driving home. I had to pull over on the side of the road to take a quick nap just so I could safely drive the rest of the way.

Losing sleep was just one of many sacrifices I had to make to provide a nice place for us to live, for Brittany's early education, and other basics. I didn't have any financial support.

My family was emotionally supportive, but you know, it's the darndest thing: when you are a child having a child, your parents are still raising their own kids. They weren't really in a position to keep up their household and their daughter's family as well. Nor did I want help. I made my bed, and by golly I was going to lie in it.

There's no making this pretty. It was ugly. I had to survive. I had to feed, educate, and clothe my daughter. I had to keep a safe roof over her head. What's more, I couldn't just sustain the status quo, because then we weren't going to get anywhere. If I was going to keep my promise to my daughter that she would have every opportunity that a child not born to a teen mom would have, I had to accelerate my success.

I even went so far as to get a tattoo as one more reminder to keep going. I had a butterfly tattooed on my hip as a symbol of rebirth. A caterpillar has to go through a lot of struggle to break through the cocoon it's trapped in, but if it endures, it breaks free as a colorful butterfly, able to fly wherever it desires.

That tattoo was there to remind me that while Brittany and I were starting over as a duo, it was going to be OK. I remember many times I would cry throughout my entire morning shower. I was exhausted—unsure where the energy would come from to get through the day, and disgusted with myself for how much I was failing at life.

Then I would get a glimpse of that butterfly tattoo and think, *We're going to freakin' do this.*

With a daily renewed resolve, I kept plugging away at it. It wasn't always so graceful; in fact, sometimes I was downright disgraceful. No one could ever hurt me again because I would be sure to beat them to it.

Surviving the teen mom trenches actually made me a better professional. It (eventually) made me better at relationships and better at "adulting" (living like a responsible adult). I got a grip on many areas of life much faster than I likely would have had I not been a young mother.

Before I learned the ins and outs of branding, promotion, leadership, or any business principle, I learned some solid life lessons.

FIGURE OUT WHAT YOU ARE GOOD AT AND THEN DO IT

Don't be bothered with what you think other people expect of you when it comes to your raw talent.

I mean, we don't have time to screw around when we're trying to make ends meet, right? I had to break into industries, figure out what it was that made people respond positively to me, and how I could get a job over somebody else. I had to quickly determine how to simultaneously get more hours assigned to me and convince employers to be flexible with me because my life was in total chaos.

By bringing my best self to the table, I was able to help solve the problems of my employers and their customers and that brought me favor.

What problems can you solve without having to force it? Without having to try to do things you are not naturally good at doing?

One day I was working at my main job when two people from a competing company came in to be nosy, quite frankly. While they were there, I took an inbound sales call. I had a smidge of training and a form to fill out for each call, but not much beyond that. However, I love the art of making relationships natural, and I like to come up with creative solutions to people's problems. So when I took that call, I just did my thing, as if I were speaking with a friend. I had no idea I was good at sales calls. I mean, I was nineteen.

To my surprise, those same two people came back the next week and offered me a job. Not just any job, but a job with benefits. I could actually insure my daughter and, if we got in a car wreck, it wouldn't instigate a financial crisis. They gave me a job that came with management training and the ability to make a commission in addition to my base salary.

The commission structure alone, which paid me more the more effort I put forth, was a huge game changer for us. All because I did what came naturally to me. I wasn't trying to impress anybody; I just did what I knew to do. The right people saw the right qualities in me, and they said, "OK, we need that in our organization." I ended up being one of the top managers in the area and had a lot of success with that company. The move helped me recover from desperation and refocused my attention on a hopeful future.

So my first big piece of advice is: *Just do you.*

The right people and opportunities will be drawn to that. (We'll come back to that point several times in this book, by the way!)

BORROW THE EXPERIENCE OF OTHERS

Can you guess what I knew as a teenager about doing adult things?

Absolutely nothing.

If you don't know how to do something, find someone who does know how to do it, and learn from them or model them.

I have so many mentors in my life, so many people I can point to and say they invested in my understanding of life. Shoot, I even had people who just plain ol' took pity on me, who didn't know me from Adam, but taught me better when they had a chance.

I remember the first time I financed a car. Praise be to God, the man who took me through that experience for the first time gently, but firmly, insisted that I pay attention to what was going on. I had a turquoise beeper and it kept distracting me as I was being repeatedly paged.

He looked at me and said, "Hey, you're about to sign your life away for five years. Why don't you put that pager up while we go through what this means for you?"

He then talked me through the agreement, what was most important to worry about, and how some car salespeople could take advantage of me in the future. He then continued to call and check on me for a few months after. He was an older gentleman, and he was concerned about my ability to handle adult decisions. He took me in just like that.

I kind of caught on at that point, so I started looking for people to show me how to do things I was clueless about. Like when I bought my first house or when I wanted to improve a specific skill, like sales or marketing.

It could be for personal things too. I was always looking for good, strong married couples because I had failed at committed relationships despite my parents being married since the beginning of time. (Well, it seems that way, anyway!)

Nobody can experience everything, so you need to borrow the experience of others, ask lots of questions, and ask for help. It instantly reduces your learning curve because you don't have to make the same mistakes others made to glean from the lessons they learned.

It's one of the key factors in my success of going from a teen mom—with a first-class ticket on the struggle bus—to being where I am today.

OWN UP TO MISTAKES

Own your mistakes. Even when you're in the process of screwing up. Remember that car I bought? Well, as I mentioned, things were tight, and no matter how much I worked, I managed to always have more month than money. So, I would be late on my payment. I mean, not sometimes. *Every single month.* I just couldn't keep up. Every so often they deferred a payment and added a payment onto the end of the loan, but outside of those glorious months, I would call them and literally read them my budget.

The conversation on my end sounded like this: "OK, this is what I have coming in this month. These are all the jobs that I work and these are the hours that I work at each job. This is what's due this week, so this is all I have to pay on my car this month because we also have to eat. I'm sorry, but I will have it to you on Friday."

And sometimes I had to call them back on Friday and explain that I ended up not making as much in tips as I expected, and I would be forty or fifty dollars short.

While the employees of the local finance company did all they could to help me, they could not always save me from the big late fees or even from myself.

It seemed as if I was always on the verge of my car being repossessed. It was—ahem—good times. So much fun back then! When it was like the absolute cutoff date to get my payment in before my car would be in jeopardy, those employees would stay late for me so I could drive an hour in traffic, hand them a payment in cash, and get it logged into the system—all so I could keep my car. It was usually down to the wire like that. I did make some stupid decisions, but again, remember, I was doing this completely on my own. Had I not been totally honest with these people, they would not have stood in the gap to ensure I averted the worst-case scenario.

That business was a business full of people with hearts, not just a bunch of robots.

And when I finally paid off that loan, I went to that location and celebrated with those people. Yes, we actually celebrated. It was that big of a deal to me. However, that celebration would have never happened if I had not owned up to my mistakes.

LOOK FOR THE RIGHT SOLUTION

If something doesn't work, try something different. Don't go ball up, cry in a corner, and say, "Woe is me." Kick yourself in the pants and force yourself to get on to the next alternative.

"Plan B" is nonsense. Successful people come up with plans A, B, C, D . . . all the way to Z. That's how life works. If you're not constantly looking for and testing solutions, that's probably why you're on the hamster wheel that you're on right now.

Back in the day, if I hit a roadblock, there was no one to catch my slack. I didn't have anybody to whom I could say, "OK, I'm tired. Pick up the ball and run with it." That's not how my life worked. If I was going to feed my kid, if I was going to provide a life for this child who was completely dependent on me, who was my entire life, I had to keep trying.

Find another solution. That's how you move toward success.

DO WHAT YOU SAY YOU'RE GOING TO DO

Follow through. You'd be surprised how many people don't do that. If you have to stay up all night to get it done, then do that. If you consistently see that you cannot actually get things done in the time frame you committed to, stop overcommitting.

When I moved out of my hometown to the far west side of Nashville, I had to leave my gym membership. According to my agreement, if you moved fifty miles or more, you could get out of your membership with a thirty-day notice. It wasn't quite fifty miles away, but regardless, I didn't give a full thirty-day notice. Technically, I was supposed to pay another month. The owner made this clear to me, and I told him I didn't have an extra thirty-nine dollars, but I would pay it as soon as I could. (I told you those days were rough.) However, I knew that I owed it, and I added that month's fee to the piece of paper I tracked my debts on.

More than a year later, I called him and said, "Hey, I just wanted to confirm that it was thirty-nine dollars I owed you for not turning in my thirty-day notice. I want to send that to you to settle up."

"Oh, Amber," he said, "I just wrote that off."

I insisted. "I made the commitment. I signed that contract. I told you I would pay it," I said, trying to do the right thing.

That impressed him, evidently. He asked me what I was doing professionally.

I told him. At that time, it was the job I got from answering the phone and having a good inbound sales call presentation.

He said, "I would love for you to interview for a sales and marketing position I have."

"Well, I am not really looking," I explained.

He persisted. "Just come talk to me. Let me tell you about it."

I reluctantly went for an official interview, then got the position.

Johnny Keel ended up being my first mentor. He not only taught me the baseline of business, he helped me shift from being a kid who had a kid to becoming a professional woman. He taught me about sales, how to influence decisions, and about business. And before he lost a valiant battle with colon cancer, he reminded everyone that any day your feet hit the ground is a great day. He never complained, no matter how sick he got. There's not a week that goes by that I don't lean on something Johnny taught me.

His wife and founder of the business, Peggy, introduced me to personal and professional development. She gave me my first personality test, sent me to conferences and trainings, and bought me books on how to network, sell, and market. She pushed me and gave me space to try new things, even if they didn't always work. It was a safe place to innovate and a safe place to fail.

I like to say that I grew up at Sports Village (the name of that upscale health club). While I was employed there, I experienced the 9/11 terrorist attacks in 2001, returned to college and completed my PR and advertising degree, had my son (who was a piece-of-cake planned C-section and a piece-of-cake baby), and had many other important experiences.

All this happened because I said I was going to do something and followed through. Had I not picked up that phone, had I avoided those circumstances, I never would have gotten that job, and my life would not have changed, for the better, so rapidly.

Now, I want to encourage you, even if you feel like you're going to look stupid: do what you say you're going to do. Even if you can't quite do it all the way, try, display the effort. People will respect you for it. And you will find so much more success if you suck it up and do what you say you're going to do. Be a person of character people can count on.

IT DOES GET BETTER, SO KEEP GOING

Broken bones heal stronger. I don't know the moment where I thought, *Oh, it's all going to be OK*, because it just seemed so intense for so long. Yet, one day it just got better.

It might have been a mental shift for me. Maybe things were better, longer, and earlier than I knew they were, but I had to believe it wasn't a fleeting season. I had to know it was a sustainable state of being.

With the promise to my daughter in clear focus—that she would have every opportunity as an adult that a child not born to a teen mom would have—I kept going. I believed if I just kept doing the right things I would get there, even if I took a few hits, on occasion, from doing the wrong things.

I want you to believe that about your life. I want you to believe that about your business. I want you to believe that about your relationships.

These lessons were butt kickers and, of course, I didn't learn them the easy way. I have to learn everything the hard way, you know, for things to stick.

The bottom line is that no matter what you've experienced in life, no matter what kind of trauma you've been through, no matter what bad decisions you've made, if you accept the realities of your situation, you can properly address them with a plan and with action.

Lucky for you, you bought a book that is slap full of advice for taking the right kinds of action with your business. Now that you know my story, it's time to get down to business. From this point forward this book is tactical and you will have homework via the "Take Action Bombshell" sections at the end of each chapter. Remember, I promised you a no-fluff-zone. Are you ready? Let's do this!

Take Action, Bombshell!

Visit www.thebombshellbusinesswoman.com for free, downloadable worksheets and resources.

1. *Write down the one thing that happened in life that still holds you back from your own greatness.* What is keeping you from really shining professionally and helping other people with your gifts and talents?

2. *List five good things that came out of that situation.* (As I did, listing several examples of how bad situations either taught me a solid life lesson or turned into opportunities for growth.) You can find those in your story too!

3. *Now, in a few sentences, write what your future is going to look like when you move past your limitations and show gratitude for the lessons they afforded you.*

four

Following Your Breadcrumbs

Often, the people I work with have a lot of confusion about who they are and who they want to become, whether it's relating to their business brand or their personal brand.

They get really stuck when I ask them, "Well, what makes you different? What makes you unique?"

Or, I have wantrepreneurs, those who want to start their own business but aren't sure what type of business to start. Each time I'm consulted I tell these ladies this: "Follow your breadcrumbs."

When you leave breadcrumbs behind when traveling a path, you can always find your way back to where you started. Life has a way of doing that for you. If you look back on your life history, you'll see that you've left breadcrumbs for yourself so that, as an adult, you can reflect and say, *Oh, OK. Here's the commonality in all of these different circumstances.*

It's kind of like choosing how to exercise as an adult. If you hated running as a kid, you're likely going to hate running for exercise. If you loved swimming as a kid, then swimming might be something you should do to stay in the habit of exercise.

In that same spirit, you can look back and know what type of work you not only consistently enjoyed, but also uniquely excelled at.

I remember having lunch with a friend who was trying to figure out what he wanted to do next in his career. He said to me, "You're just like the Madonna of business. How do you keep reinventing yourself?"

"Well, I don't," I answered. "I've done the same thing over and over and over again at the core. It's just dressed differently each time."

I explained to him that communication and engagement is my jam. Because I know that so well, it doesn't matter how that looks in my business or in my career because the same principles and skill sets apply. I can thrive in that because I inherently know how to do it.

So allow me to walk you down my memory lane so you can consider where you might look for your own breadcrumbs.

One of my earliest memories of understanding the importance of engagement was when I was very young—like four years old. I was a part of a Christian church version of the Girl Scouts. It was very cliquish and they did stupid things I couldn't have cared less about.

I remember one night they painted everybody's toenails, hid a few of the girls behind a shower curtain, and then the larger group voted for whose toenails were best.

While I'm all about a pedicure now, at four years old I was a rough and tumble little girl—a tomboy, really. I just wanted to be in the real deal (not some generic version) of the Boy Scouts anyway. I mean, they were learning how to make fires and how to tell the difference between coyote poop and domestic dog poop. Way more fun.

Worst of all, as I said, the group was cliquish. There was no feeling of belonging or warm welcome to new girls, and I'm a belonging kind of girl. I have never had a hard time making friends, but even at that early age I was like, *Yeah, I don't want to be like you people. You're not my tribe.*

See? That's a breadcrumb. (An early one.) My entire career has been about communication and engagement. Even at a prekindergarten age, I knew that was important to me; I could read this at the level a four-year-old could intellectually process.

Now, let's fast-forward a bit to junior high when I went to Southern California Christian Junior High and High School, a small private school with a lot of love but limited resources. The high school had an official yearbook, but the junior high did not, so my three best girlfriends—Wendy, Emily, and Jaime—and I decided to create a yearbook ourselves. We collected photos, surveyed classmates, came up with funny things to say about our peers, conducted a superlatives process, photocopied pop culture references out of teen magazines, and more.

As eighth-graders we simply wanted to share what our last year of junior high was like. We wanted to make everybody feel a part of that eighth-grade class, so we decided to literally copy and paste together, then photocopy, a yearbook for our classmates. We figured if we did all the work, we could convince the administration to allow us access to the school photocopier, which they did.

We rocked that out, working together to make something special. It was a ball. I still have that photocopied yearbook. My friends and I wanted so badly to communicate and engage, whether we knew that's what we were doing at the time or not. It's a great memory. And another breadcrumb.

Later on, I was what they called a sophomore executive at

Lebanon High School in Tennessee. A far ways from Southern California Christian Junior High and High School, again, I just wanted to do something to bring our class together. I also knew we had a lot of cool people in our class and that our cliques intermingled, unlike some of the other classes.

I remember sitting in the office of our principal, Mr. Malone, presenting our case that we should have a school-sponsored sophomore lock-in. Then I went and convinced my church that they should allow Lebanon High to use our basketball gym as the location.

But I didn't stop there. I convinced my youth group leader that he should allow us to use the sound system he rented for another youth event so we could have a big dance-sounding, club-type experience.

Somehow, countless parents thought it was a good idea to let their fourteen- to sixteen-year-old kids hang out in a church gym all night long—and what's even crazier is some of those parents were convinced to chaperone.

The event was well attended and everyone had a blast. Again, this took a lot of communication and engagement. Our student council representatives had to work together to do all this convincing of decision-makers, we had to promote the event, and then we had to make the experience worth talking about.

At our ten-year reunion, classmates were still talking about that experience—how fun it was, and how it sent us on a trajectory of being a tight-knit class.

You can call that a fond high school memory. I call it a breadcrumb. Once again, it required effective communication and a ton of engagement among many different types of people.

Finally, when I was around eighteen, I was second assistant manager at the local Fashion Bug. It was my first management role and I felt a huge amount of responsibility, even though second assistant manager only amounted to me being "third key," or another human who could unlock the door and the register. I didn't actually manage anyone or anything, but that didn't matter! I was management!

That's why when Hibbett Sports moved into the location beside us, I gathered up funds from all of us Fashion Bug girls and got them a "welcome to the shopping center" present. With our gift in hand, we waltzed into their sports store, offered our welcomes, shared how we handled our shoplifters, and encouraged them to reach out if they needed anything.

What followed was a great business-to-business relationship and even a lot of fun. Whether we were planning joint promotions or playing practical jokes on each other, we created a community within our shopping center that made coming to work enjoyable—and all our jobs easier.

So you can pass this experience off as a simple hourly college job. Or you can dig a little deeper and see the breadcrumb that again points back to a natural inclination and gift for communication and engagement.

As you can see, before I knew the direction of my career, I knew I wanted people to feel a part of something bigger. I instinctively created experiences that made people feel like they belonged and had friends—they were part of a tribe—and oh, we're going to have a lot of fun.

Eventually, I decided to go back to college and get my public relations degree so I could learn all of this for realies. I built on this obvious area of focus through multiple entrepreneurial and employment adventures.

Fast-forward to my last actual job. I was on the human resources leadership team for Gaylord Opryland Resort and Attractions, the largest Marriott hotel in the world.

Of course, my entire gig was . . . you guessed it . . .

communication and engagement. It was my job to oversee the department that focused on the happiness of our 3,000 employees. My team produced everything from newsletters to video spoofs to back-of-the-house television announcements to small meetings and awards luncheons. For good measure, we did large-scale full-production events with indoor pyrotechnics, stilt walkers, break dancers, and more.

Through company-wide communication, events, recognition, and more, our internal public relations team ensured that everyone saw how their contributions fit into the big picture, thereby increasing employee satisfaction and ultimately the commitment to the brand's goals and customer experience.

I personally worked with the senior leaders on their personal brands as an internal publicist so they could effectively influence their teams. Together we gave emerging leaders and department heads all the support they needed so these same strategies would trickle downward among their teams. In the end, this allowed us to rock guest satisfaction at the Opryland Hotel and its attractions.

Now as a speaker, consultant, and author, I teach these things to the masses. I teach small businesses how to communicate and engage with their customers and teams. When I enter corporate environments, I teach managers how to communicate and engage with their employees.

So it's crystal clear to me what I do best and can get paid for—thanks to my breadcrumbs.

Now I want you to go back to when you were four. Then junior high and high school. What memories do you most treasure? What was the common thread in all of your jobs, even if it wasn't the core of your job?

For example, if you were amazing at bringing people together for volunteer work, that might be something you need to pay attention to. Maybe you need to position your business to work with nonprofits.

If you were the person who could not stand to look at her friend's cluttered closet—so you tore it apart and put it all back together—that could be a clue that you may excel in a business that demands organizational skill. Or perhaps your existing business can be known for being exceptionally efficient, giving you a competitive advantage.

So, now it's your turn. I want you to take a walk down memory lane. Consider the decisions you've made over your lifetime. In doing so, you will reveal undeniable commonalities that will allow you to connect the dots. Then let the breadcrumbs of your journey help you find your way "back home" today, and move you in a strategic direction tomorrow.

This direction will be based on your highest value, what you want to be known for, and what you can joyfully do day in and day out for a living while operating in your greatest gift.

You actually get to say, "Hey, here's my awesome gift that I was designed to do in this life. This is the one I've done successfully my entire life to this point and I'm going to share that with you. In exchange, you're going to thank me by giving me money."

Then you can feel good about that exchange because you're not second-guessing yourself, you're not feeling like a fraud, and you're not feeling like you're operating in a way that's frustrating. It's powerful to finally have the "Aha!" moment, when you realize, *Man, this is what I should be doing.*

Take Action, Bombshell!

Visit www.thebombshellbusinesswoman.com for free, downloadable worksheets and resources.

1. *List five words that describe your greatest gifts or talents.*

2. *Take a walk down memory lane: recount memories that reveal a combined passion and talent of yours that produced a positive result in each season of your life. Remember not to limit yourself to stories directly related to your role at the time. Think out of the box!*

   Elementary school:

   Junior high/middle school:

   High school:

   College or college age:

   Relevant work experiences (perhaps limit these to your favorite jobs or businesses):

3. *What roles do you play with family and friends at this point in your life?* (the organizer, host, counselor, etc.)

4. *List three words that describe how you feel in those situations.*

5. *List three words that describe how you make other people feel in those situations.*

6. *List the common skills that you consistently use in each of those situations.*

7. *Now, after reflecting on your memories and accomplishments, state what you discovered are your areas of expertise. Use one or two sentences.*

8. *How can this information help you focus your current business or understand what type of business you should launch?*

five

The Bombshell Business Dictionary

One of the things I hear women say repeatedly that drives me nuts is, "I'm really good at what I do, but I'm not a good businesswoman."

The crazy thing is, when I ask them what defines a "good businesswoman," they have no real definition. They just say they know they are not it.

According to auditor giant KPMG's 2015 Women's Leadership Study, 63 percent of women surveyed said confidence was a top characteristic of a leader, but only 49 percent said they were confident at the time of the survey. But at least that's an improvement from how they felt when they were growing up, since only 31 percent said they were confident as children![1]

It's no wonder today's fempreneurs don't see themselves for exactly who they are when they are dealing with decades of insecurity! Yet it's not just new female business owners who lack confidence; it's successful women in business too.

In 2014 I chaired the Nashville ATHENA PowerLink® (APL) Advisory Program, which was designed to increase the growth and profitability of women-owned businesses. The program matches a woman business owner in their respective cities with a team of successful volunteer advisors for a year of mentoring. This advisory panel deep dives into her business, determines the steps she needs to take in order to grow, then meets with her multiple times through the year to ensure she has the support she needs to do it.

What woman business owner meeting the basic qualifications would pass up this opportunity? I was baffled by a low application number.

While trying to overcome this low application rate, I found that the number one objection to applying was that the six-figure business owners I approached were concerned they could not put together the required business plan to accompany their application, nor were they comfortable opening up their books to our governing body, which selected the candidates each year.

In response to these concerns, the immediate past chair and I hosted a lunch and learn. I presented the extreme benefits of the program, made the business language more approachable, and handed out ready-made forms I designed to simplify the business plan and financial reporting process.

Not only did we receive quality applicants that year, but the Nashville APL governing body selected two candidates for the first time since there were two extremely strong contenders.

To be clear, I'm not suggesting that women need business principles dumbed down. Perhaps the problems are awareness and access.

According to the US Women's Chamber of Commerce, factors that hold women back and contribute to their estimated

$10 trillion-dollar opportunity loss include lack of access to mainstream business education, lack of access to capital, and not enough mentoring.[2]

From my experience, though, the only difference I see between men and women in business is that men are more likely to leap, then figure out the rest as they go. Women tend to consistently undervalue their experience and abilities. (Of course, if women were not routinely projected as objects instead of contributing thinkers and doers, things might shake out differently. But that's another book entirely.)

For women and men alike who might be overcomplicating things, allow me to show you how simple business can be at its most basic levels.

DEFINING YOUR BUSINESS

Business acumen is something that evolves with time and experience, but the reality is most small business owners won't be throwing around the same terms Fortune 100s use in their quarterly earnings calls. That's why I created my own language to use with my Bombshells. I invite you to use the following to keep it real, and I encourage you to use the concepts, but perhaps not the exact terms, with your banker!

Let's start with the definition of business. Fist bump to all the Harvard MBA fancy-pants who can articulately and thoroughly define the concept of a business. Please cover your eyes while I simplify the idea via the business-according-to-Amber Hurdle definition, found in the Bombshell Business Dictionary.

Business: *When an individual or group of individuals solve customer problems in exchange for money.*

Women own 35.95 percent of all US firms, yet only 4.82

percent of all revenues are produced from those firms, according to the 2012 Survey of Business Owners conducted by the US Census Bureau.[3]

First, let's put an emphasis on the "in exchange for money" part.

Let's be clear here: *Ain't nobody gonna separate from their cold hard cash unless they have an unresolved problem,* so if you want to make money, you have to be incredibly clear about what problem(s) you solve.

Rabbi Lapin describes money as "certificates of appreciation" in *Thou Shall Prosper: Ten Commandments for Making Money.* So listen up, Bombshells: your natural gifts are meant to serve other people. You can use the gifts you have, ones others don't have, to solve their problems in exchange for those little certificates of appreciation.

Not only is that OK—it's expected. So stop undervaluing yourself.

What exact problem *do* you solve? How much does it cost you to solve the problem? How much do you charge to solve the problem?

That's your business.

Do you fancy yourself a "goddess guide for heart-centered exercisers"?

No, ma'am. You're a yoga instructor.

Think that you are a "scissor-wielding-style architect" whose talents cannot be confined to an oppressive existing business category?

Guess what, Sister. The US Small Business Association isn't going to give you a loan because there is no North American Industry Classification System (NAICS) code assigned to that nonexistent category. Nor is that category available when you register for online business listings.

There are ample opportunities to express your creativity in

business. Explaining the function of your business is not one of them, so leave your unicorns in their stalls for this part.

Be clear about what it is you do, and you will find it becomes clear who your competition is, how to market your business, what resources are available to you, and what type of complementary businesses can help you succeed faster.

Speaking of clarity, that brings me to my next Bombshell Business Dictionary definition.

YOUR BUSINESS MOJO

Many budding Bombshell are multipassionate and want to offer everything to everybody. They want to express every talent they ever had and please every person who gives them an idea (whether or not that person is a viable potential customer). They let insecurity and doubt drive decisions instead of using confidence in the problems they uniquely solve and the people they uniquely serve.

Instead of focusing and becoming known for something great, they generalize and aren't known for anything special, which decreases the number of potential customers they can acquire and reduces both customer loyalty and repeat sales.

It is *very* easy to get excited about bright, shiny objects when you are an entrepreneur. We have more ideas than we can ever execute. So how do you decide what to prioritize and what to let go?

You have to find your Business Mojo.

Your Business *Mojo*

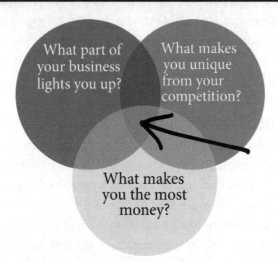

What part of your business lights you up?

What makes you unique from your competition?

What makes you the most money?

*Your **Business Mojo** is an internal statement that guides the focus of your business model where the answers to these three questions overlap.*

1. *What part of your business lights you up?*
   Meaning: what do you get really excited about and find yourself working on when you "should be" doing other things?

2. *What makes you unique from your competition?*
   Really, what can you do better than everyone else, or what can only be said about you? Don't be vanilla here!

3. *What makes you the most money?*
   When you pull out your sales from the past three to twelve months, what product or services made you the most *profit*? In other words, what puts the most cash in your pocket?

This is not a statement you promote to your customers.

Rather, it is an internal reminder of how you are going to go about pursuing your company mission. It should be used to drive your team toward offering your highest value while keeping you off the many entrepreneurial rabbit trails you will be tempted with.

You may find that you are passionate about some things, but no one wants to pay you for that passion. Or you may find you make a lot of money selling something, but you dread creating it. Or you might be unique in some way from your competition, but you can't find a way to leverage that unique attribute to really make money.

Your business is what you do. To find out how to take the actions you need to make the most money with the least amount of resistance, you have to overlap all three areas of the Business Mojo equation.

So what does this overlap look like in a real business?

Renae Keller's business is interior design. Her clients' problem is that they need the interior decorative elements of their space designed. However, knowing that alone does not help her focus her daily operations, so we broke down the process for Renae Keller Interior Design's Business Mojo Statement like this (following the formula).

WHAT PART OF YOUR BUSINESS LIGHTS YOU UP?

Renae thrives on walking into a vast abyss of ideas and opportunities, then tailoring a detailed plan based on the family's unique functional needs and its story.

WHAT MAKES YOU UNIQUE FROM YOUR COMPETITION?

Some designers claim they are detail-oriented, and maybe compared to the average, they are. Renae, however, is next-level "how did she even think of that" attentive to detail. Yet she does not do it in a neurotic, mad artist type of way. She does it to delight her clients so they can live in what they specifically consider their haven.

No matter where you turn in a RKID-designed home, there are nuances that reflect the people who live there, from practical (yet beautiful) solutions to support the homeowner's lifestyle to well-appointed design elements that show their travels, their family history, their priorities, and, of course, their combined personal style. She ties design elements into the smallest opportunities that many designers would simply gloss over. When you think RKID, you think functional beauty by way of details.

WHAT MAKES YOU THE MOST MONEY?

Renae quickly moves beyond being a homeowner's interior designer and resource provider to becoming friends with everyone she works with. Since there is so much trust built during the sometimes stressful process of new construction or remodeling, RKID's calming presence and sure-footed experience creates clients who tend to be long-term customers. They come back to her and her team for their future projects, their children's, or parent's projects, and they refer their friends and neighbors as well. They would not dream of trusting another designer when she so clearly "gets" them. This long-term relationship minimizes the amount of client acquisition RKID has to invest in, thus increasing her profit by reducing marketing expenses and time spent studying the needs of her customers.

Once Renae found the answers to these questions, we combined them into a concise Business Mojo statement:

Renae Keller Interior Design translates a big-picture design into "every last dang detail" of a home for homeowners who engage in a long-term relationship.

Now when she makes decisions for her business, if they don't align with those priorities, she is better able to prioritize and gravitate toward that which will serve her company and, therefore, her customers. Likewise, she is better equipped to turn down opportunities.

If Renae split her focus and started to redesign doctors' offices and childcare facilities while she was also designing higher-end homes, imagine how much she would have to split her time and energy with research, shopping, and understanding the ins and outs of how to apply her love for detail into these various opportunities. It would be maddening!

Or, what if every time a stranger called Renae to help pick out paint colors, and nothing more, she took time away from her customers who needed her to calm a storm with a wayward contractor? Losing focus from her Business Mojo does not leverage her company's highest value: taking the big picture and dialing it down to tiny details that delight. She would lose both money and her sanity.

If you're feeling spread thin, if you can't figure out why you are working so hard but don't have the financial results to show for it, or if you have simply lost that loving feeling for your business altogether, it might be because you've lost your mojo!

Now that you're confident you are, in fact, a businesswoman, and you have the system to figure out how to maximize your potential as a business through a business model, let's talk about what layers you need to establish to find success.

YOUR BUSINESS SUCCESS PYRAMID

Like any building, a business demands a strong foundation to sustain storms and environmental factors that could otherwise make it collapse. The materials used on top of that foundation also determine its longevity and enjoyment.

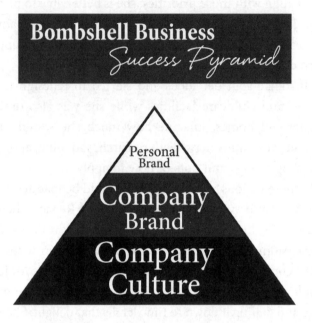

My **Business Success Pyramid** establishes your company culture as the foundation of your business—upon which your company brand rests—and then supports your personal brand and the personal brands of your team members.

If you have these three components solid in your business, you can find success if you get in there and grind until you are winning. I'll cover the ins and outs of each layer in the following chapters.

So, to recap: we've defined business in a clear way, focused our business models via the Business Mojo formula, and determined the basic layers we need in our business to grow a business via the Business Success Pyramid.

Now it's time to apply your learning.

Take Action, Bombshell!

Visit www.thebombshellbusinesswoman.com for free, downloadable worksheets and resources.

1. *Define your business. What problem do you solve in exchange for money?*

2. *Answer the following questions to explore your specific business model.*

    What part of your business lights you up?
    What makes you unique from your competition?
    What makes you the most money?

3. *Now find where the overlap exists in those three answers and write your Business Mojo statement here.*

Six

Establishing Your Company Culture

If I asked you, "What's your number one marketing challenge?" how would you answer me?

"I don't have enough money."

"I keep attracting price-sensitive customers."

"My social media sucks."

"I'm not making enough money to justify the time and expense invested in my marketing efforts."

Or maybe it's all of the above.

What if I told you your number one marketing challenge is actually *none* of the above?

I've been teaching branding and marketing for quite some time now, and I know a thing or two from repeatedly helping female entrepreneurs, with businesses like yours, who struggle to attract and retain the customers they need to make the kind of money they desire.

So if their number one marketing challenge has nothing to

do with all those frustrations, what is it?

It comes down to the lack of a really solid company culture. Simple as that.

Well, maybe it's not so simple, if you have to figure out what you as a business owner are all about, what your business wants to be known for, how you are going to manage the business you do get with the right kinds of processes, how to make sure your employees treat the business as carefully as you do, and so on.

All businesses begin and end with their company culture. Your culture is the birthplace of your brand. It keeps you focused on the business you dreamed you would operate. No matter how much your business grows, you can always come back to that original foundation to make wise decisions, attract and retain the right employees who are like-minded, and ultimately create incredible customer experiences.

When you think about company culture, you may think about Zappos, Google, or other big brands that are well noted in the news for the strength of their culture. However, no business is too small to ensure everyone who interacts with your business sings the same culture song. If this foundational piece of the Business Success Pyramid is not developed, your brand, and even your personal brand, will suffer.

What the heck is *culture*, anyway? Here it is: social norms, or, common ways of life.

When you think about Southern culture in the US, that's very different from Southern Californian culture. If you're in the South, you know that people "sit a spell," you can order sweet tea at a restaurant, and SEC football is the next most important part of life after Jesus. Those things are just understood.

Try ordering a sweet tea at a Southern California restaurant, and they will bring you a pack of sweetener. "Game day" dresses are not gracing the fronts of L.A. boutiques throughout the fall, and there's a reason why Cracker Barrel Old Country Store restaurants created a Southern dictionary for their guests to help decode things for those just passing through the Southeast.

One culture is not better than the other; they are simply different. Therefore, these cultures attract different types of people who hold the same things important.

You want to create an experience—a feeling. It's how you do business. A living, breathing company culture entails those things you do that you don't have to think about doing. You want how you do business to be consistent among all team members, including partners, management, employees, and even vendors.

Your company culture is made up of the family rules of your business that establish consistent expectations among all.

When you attempt to find a right fit for your company culture, whether it's a new employee or a new vendor, it's kind of like when you were dating and about to meet your significant other's family.

That's when you start to notice similarities or differences that can make or break "happily ever after."

Maybe in your family, Christmas is celebrated on Christmas Day, but in your significant other's family, Christmas Eve is the big deal. Maybe in your family, when you go on vacation, everybody shares a big house and it's a big to-do of togetherness. However, when your significant other's family vacations, they stay in a hotel with separate rooms for all.

Maybe your family members didn't yell at each other much. Then you fall in love with this other person and you find out their family members say mean things to each other without thinking anything of it, and screaming at each other is standard at family gatherings.

That's when you're like, *Whoa. I don't know if my family values and my family norms can fit with this crazy family that vacations differently, celebrates holidays differently, and talks to each other very differently than mine does.*

You start to think about your future and whether you can see yourself fitting, for the long term, into how this other family does life.

Now that you've got that everyday life experience in your mind, think about your employee base. Consider the way they do business, the way they do life, what their values are, how they perceive situations, and what they think is appropriate behavior and inappropriate behavior.

I bet you are thinking of someone right now who worked for you before and did not work out, not because they didn't do their job well, but because they did not jive with your company culture, whether it was spelled out or not.

Likewise, you may recall saying after an interview, "This person just feels like a right fit," even if their resume didn't totally line up with the job description. That is company culture. That person had attitudes and beliefs that naturally fit with your culture. When you have a very strong company culture, you can automatically identify those right fits. The *what to do* can be taught; the *how to do it* is not as easy to pass on to someone who simply doesn't "get it." For example, you can teach someone to run a cash register, but you can't teach someone to smile through all customer interactions.

These examples of an employee perfect fit or an employee struggle are similar to the dating example. The people you attract to your business either share how you do business "family life" or they don't. You have decide if your ways of doing business are in alignment enough with this prospective employee to say "I do" to an employee relationship.

In the same way, if you want to retain the best and the brightest, you better ensure you sustain that mutual expectation. Unfortunately, one in two employees who leave their jobs voluntarily are actually quitting their bosses, not their jobs, according to a 2015 Gallup report.[1]

As we can see, it's a two-way street.

Your company culture is the internal foundation on which everything in your business builds. To be clear, your culture is not your brand. Your brand is what your customers and potential customers think about you; your culture is who you say you are and how you do business.

When you have a strong company culture it will shine through your brand and you can authentically say, "This is what our brand is about." And you'll see that people actually believe this about you.

While I call myself a brand consultant, my secret is that I'm actually a company culture expert who carries a culture through to the branding experience from messaging to visual branding. I just cannot promote myself that way because small businesses don't get the term culture, or its impact, like they do the term *branding*. So I sell them what they want, then give them what they need.

When I'm called in to work on a rebrand, a brand clarity project, or even to launch a new brand, I always work from the inside out. What my customers realize is that when they get extremely clear on their business personality, their family rules, and how they do business, the whole marketing thing becomes a straightforward experience. It eliminates the frustration and compounding expense of marketing vendors (graphic designers, website designers, photographers, ad sales professionals, etc.) who struggle to tell the brand story in a way that satisfies the business owner and resonates with customers. It frees the business owners to delegate marketing and customer service to their team members because everyone is playing by the same rules and can represent the heart of the company as well as the owner.

And while I may come in to facilitate a brand experience, what happens is owners or managers realize that their inconsistent culture has created a chain reaction of problems, from employee practices to customer service. So we have to address many aspects of the business to prepare for success once the marketing plan starts to make the phones ring.

If the foundation of your house is falling apart, you wouldn't invite guests over, right? The same thing goes with your business. Inviting new customers into a shaky cultural foundation is a recipe for disaster operationally, and the customer experience will suffer as well.

While your company culture is the part of your business that is capable of creating sunshine and unicorns, it is also the forensic UV light of your business that can reveal things as unsettling as any crime drama episode. However, the good news is that when you know the truth, you can start to solve the mystery of what really happened and how you can make things better in the future.

A company culture generally has the following elements:

- **Company Mission Statement.** What the overall purpose of your company is. This statement should guide goal setting and decision-making, as well as provide a path to follow for all key stakeholders. Your mission statement is your North Star.

- **Company Vision.** What you want your company to aspire to and accomplish in the future. Like your mission statement, it helps keep you on track as you choose your course of action in various scenarios.

- **Company Values.** Remembering not to choose too many, so you and your staff can recall them quickly, list the top five to seven values that your business will use to guide how you do business with your customers, external partners, and employees.
- **Service Standards.** These statements should not only set the standard for your operational excellence, they should also inspire and empower team members—and beyond— to meet a level of service for your customers and each other. Again, resist the temptation to create too many. You want them to be easily remembered by your staff.

When we dive into employee practices later in the book, we will talk about how you plan to directly and indirectly communicate your cultural basics to your team, outside partners, and even your customers; how to recognize behaviors and actions that reflect and strengthen the integrity of your company culture; and, of course, how to lean on your culture when you have an opportunity to correct behaviors that don't align with your culture.

"But, Amber, it's just me," you might be saying. "I don't have employees. Do I still need a culture?"

Heavens yes!

When you create a company culture, you are drawing your lines in the sand for you, first, and then for anyone else who does business with you. It's likely that you are an entrepreneur because it gives you freedom: time freedom, creative freedom, freedom from answering to the less experienced, emotionally immature boss you used to report to. Well, consider your company culture as the constitution for your business. You are the president and these are your rules. Oh, and not only should you honor the principles upon which your business was founded, you should expect anyone else who wants to live in your world to do the same.

So instead of constantly saying, "I don't know what to do" or, "I don't know if this is a good decision for my business," you can—with boldness—be decisive and know that you are moving in the direction you intended for your business upon its creation. Instead of agreeing to something that doesn't sit right with your spirit, you can simply say, "That's not in line with my company vision, but thank you for the opportunity."

Still not convinced?

According to an article published by Deloitte University Press, 50 percent of survey respondents claimed company culture, engagement, and employee retention are top challenges for leaders, as opposed to only 20 percent who said the same the prior year.[2]

When you consider that the US Small Business Administration claims small businesses have provided 55 percent of all jobs and 66 percent of all net new jobs since the 1970s, it's obvious that even small businesses can no longer ignore fostering and leading a company culture in favor of operations-only management.[3]

Creating a company culture is the first operational step in becoming a bold, brave fempreneur. It creates certainty, a road map, and stability.

So, are you ready to define your company culture? In the following chapter, I'll walk through cultural basics and share big-business examples so you can identify with businesses you know about.

Take Action, Bombshell!

*Visit www.thebombshellbusinesswoman.com for free,
downloadable worksheets and resources.*

1. *Describe your business's "way of life." How do you want customers, team members, and vendors to feel when they interact with your business?*

2. *Make a list of companies you enjoy doing business with, then describe what that experience is like. How can you create that type of experience in your business?*

3. *If you already have pieces or all of these components of your company culture in place, write them below for future reference before we go deeper in the next chapter.*

Seven

Defining Your Mission, Vision, Values, and Service Standards

In the Bombshell Business Dictionary, we defined what a business is so you can be clear with everyone what it is your business functionally does.

Now it's time to declare your mission, vision, values, and service standards.

COMPANY MISSION

Your mission statement outlines why your company exists. It doesn't have to be all fancy-pants, just a clear statement of what you do.

Knowing your "why" is important because: it will keep you focused on the goal you set for your company; it provides clear direction to employees and allows them to see how their job function fits into the big picture, keeping them engaged; and it should clarify your focus for your customers, prospects, industry professionals, and the media.

The popular social media channel Pinterest says, "Our *mission* is to help people discover the things they love and inspire them to go do those things in their daily lives."

Someone who wants to help people become more creative in their everyday lives would likely be drawn to that mission as a potential employee. When things get stressful and the work of the mission gets tough, a clear mission enables employees to take a step back and remember why they are committed in the first place. It connects them to a higher purpose than the tactical to-dos of the day. It shows the value of their work in a way that is bigger than themselves or their individual contributions. They are part of something significant, whether they are writing code, cleaning offices, or making executive decisions.

Your business may not be remotely near the size of Pinterest (yet), but it was only possible for Pinterest to grow into the pop culture phenomenon it is today because of the many people who decided their work could contribute to the mission, folks who determined to perform at a higher level to ensure the company's success.

VISION STATEMENT

While a mission statement speaks to why a company exists, a vision statement communicates what you want to accomplish in the future. It is a clear strategy to work toward.

I'll use one of my favorite brands, American Express, as an example, as they have extraordinary customer service.

It's no coincidence that they are also so proud of their culture that they post it right on their website. Their vision statement says: "We work every day to make American Express the world's most respected service brand."[1]

To do that, they created a company culture that employees

could lean on to provide "exceptional service" to their customers.

See how they wrapped up their entire hope for their future in the strength of their culture? I told you it was important!

No matter the situation, every American Express employee knows who the company aspires to be, and they understand every interaction they have with their customers and each other should reflect that. Likewise, customers, media, and business partners look to American Express as the standard of customer service.

Imagine the doors of opportunity that swing wide open in light of that reputation. Imagine the doors of opportunity that can swing wide open for you if your vision is clear, well communicated, and upheld by everyone who represents your company?

CORE VALUES

Collectively, your values are the measuring stick for how you make decisions in your business: goal setting, employee conduct, recognition, discipline—everything. They are the philosophies that your business operates on in order to support your vision. If a decision doesn't align with your values, it's a no-go. Trust and loyalty are built through this common set of unifying standards.

While you can post these values publicly, as many large organizations do, it is most important to define each value with your internal audience in mind first and foremost. Yes, it is cool that your customers and prospects can learn about your culture. However, it is vital that how you make your decisions is as clear to your employees (or future employees) as it is to you. That's why each value should be plainly and concisely defined in a sentence or two.

Remember, the more values you claim to have and the longer their definitions, the less likely your employees can quickly remember them when they need to lean on them during a normal business day.

Less is more. Keep that in mind as you create, recreate, or refine your company's list of values, as with anything else. For example, it is not necessary to list both "honesty" and "integrity" in a set of values. If you are a person of integrity, you will naturally be honest.

Let's again look to American Express, which calls their value statements their Blue Box Values. They reflect who they are and what they stand for. They include:

- Customer commitment

- Quality

- Integrity

- Teamwork

- Respect for people

- Good citizenship

- A will to win

- Personal accountability

Each of these values has a brief description, which you can view at http://about.americanexpress.com/oc/whoweare. You will see how brief each clarifying statement is, which helps team members recall the intent of the value without having to remember a bunch of flowery words.

As you can see, if American Express has the vision to be the world's most respected service brand, these are the things they must hold valuable in their day-to-day operations, throughout all decision-making, and in all business interactions.

Consider how values like these can act as a lighthouse for you or your team, no matter how choppy the waters get or how dark the sky becomes.

For example, have you ever heard someone say, "Well, that's not my job"?

Uh . . . yeah, it is.

Every single person who represents your company represents your brand. Every problem a customer has is every team member's problem. Whether they have the authority or knowledge to fix problems is irrelevant. They are the key to finding the solution.

With that in mind, it's no wonder a company that wants to be the most respected service brand values "teamwork" enough to include it in its documented cultural basics.

Let's say a customer calls a day spa during the afternoon shift to book a service, but has special requirements due to allergies. She needs to know about the ingredients in the products that will be used during her upcoming body treatment, but since the vendor who sold the body treatment supplies to the spa is closed for the day, the afternoon shift's front desk manager tells the customer someone will call her the next day. So she leaves a note for the morning staff—but no one follows up.

In fact, the morning front desk manager decides it is not her customer inquiry, she can't quickly find the vendor's contact information, and she does not want to deal with a "high maintenance guest" on the phone anyway. She decides it can wait until the afternoon manager comes in again.

The only problem is, the afternoon manager's son becomes ill and, without a babysitter, she is unable to work her shift. Service providers cover the front desk in between treatments, nervously using the computer system and praying they don't mess anything up. They certainly aren't thinking about yesterday's customer follow-up.

In one decision made by one team member who did not share the value of teamwork, a ball got dropped.

Come to find out, the customer with sensitive skin planned to try out the spa out upon recommendation of a current customer because she was told it was the perfect place to host her fifteen-person bachelorette party.

Yet, what woman in her right mind would invite her closest friends for the most important event in her life to a spa that could not be bothered with letting her know if the treatment she wanted to try was safe for her skin?

What's worse, an existing happy customer now has a negative experience associated with the spa because her referral ended up being a dud in the eyes of her friend.

The owner and service providers miss out on revenue; bad word of mouth circulates, keeping others from becoming new customers; trust is broken with a current customer; and a potential long-term customer is lost for good—all because one employee did not value teamwork.

This happens in businesses everywhere, every day.

What's worse is that business owners, who are naturally tenacious, accountable, and driven, assume anyone they employ will share their value of teamwork.

Sorry, Sister. You are not "normal." You are exceptional. You are a Bombshell. If this was easy, everyone would be a successful business owner.

That's why you have to spell out everything you expect and only include people in your world who are willing to buy into that philosophy.

Your sanity—and your business checking account—will thank you.

If you need help identifying values for your company, take a look at this table and see if anything resonates.

VALUES INVENTORY

Accountability	Equality	Perseverance
Accuracy	Ethics	Power
Achievement	Excellence	Preparedness
Adaptability	Exploration	Recognition
Adventurousness	Family	Reliability
Ambition	Fitness	Resourcefulness
Assertiveness	Focus	Respect
Awareness	Freedom	Responsibility
Balance	Friendships	Rigor
Beauty	Fun	Risk-taking
Belonging	Generosity	Safety
Boldness	Goodness	Security
Calmness	Grace	Self-discipline
Carefulness	Growth	Self-reliance
Caring	Happiness	Selflessness
Challenge	Hard work	Serenity
Cheerfulness	Health	Service
Commitment	Honor	Simplicity
Compassion	Humility	Spontaneity
Competition	Humor	Stability
Consistency	Independence	Strength
Courage	Ingenuity	Success
Creativity	Initiative	Support
Curiosity	Insightfulness	Teamwork
Decisiveness	Integrity	Thankfulness
Dependability	Intuition	Thoughtfulness
Determination	Joy	Timeliness
Dignity	Justice	Tradition
Diligence	Leadership	Trust
Discipline	Legacy	Understanding
Diversity	Listening	Uniqueness
Effectiveness	Love	Unity
Efficiency	Loyalty	Usefulness
Elegance	Mastery	Vision
Empathy	Originality	Vitality
Energy	Patience	Well-being
Enthusiasm	Patriotism	Wellness
Environmental	Peace	Zeal

SERVICE STANDARDS

There is no better industry than the hospitality business to model how to impeccably establish service standards. Service standards create the standard of expectation that you and all team members follow when interacting with customers.

The Ritz-Carlton has an internationally recognized company culture that is the foundation of its iconic luxury brand. (Remember the Business Success Pyramid?) This culture is so well-revered that even nonhospitality brands flock to the Ritz-Carlton Leadership Center, which offers outside organizations an opportunity to learn their way of doing business through courses, speakers, and consulting services.

The Ritz-Carlton culture, which the company refers to as its Gold Standards, can be found on its website at http://www.ritzcarlton.com/en/about/gold-standards.

Within their culture are their own service standards. They start with three steps of service, which include these basic courtesies. I have paraphrased them below and added my commentary.

1. Greet the customer sincerely (in person or on the phone, whether a guest or a fellow employee).

2. Use the customer's name (there is no sound sweeter to an individual than their own name) and know what they might need before even they do, and make it happen. (Like a server filling your water glass before it's empty, exceptional service should always anticipate the needs of customers.)

3. Warmly say good-bye. (This is your last impression. Make it count.)

Simple. You acknowledge this person using their name, anticipate what they might need, and make sure they feel good when they leave.

However, if it's that simple, why is it that your boutique's part-time sales associate lets customers walk out your business doors without saying, "Thanks for shopping with us. Hope to see you again soon!"

Isn't it obvious that is how things should happen?

Not so much.

Differences in personalities, generations, cultures, and more bring a variety of experiences, expectations, perceptions, and behaviors to you and your team. What might be an obvious way of doing business to one individual might be foreign to another.

So what are those very basic expectations you have of yourself, whether you are a solopreneur (solo entrepreneur) or if you have a team of employees?

A common service standard in the retail industry is, "Stop, drop, and greet." Meaning, within ten seconds of a customer walking through the door, it is expected that team members will stop whatever it is they are doing, drop whatever it is they are working on, and welcome that person to their store.

Make your service standards easy to remember, just like your mission, vision, and values. Yes, I said that your culture is your company's constitution, but you don't want it to read like one!

The Ritz-Carlton takes it a step further and has several service values (which you can explore on their website). You may find it helpful to expand on the super basic to further explain, based on your industry and customer base, what your nonnegotiable customer service standards are.

If you do have a team, it is also important that if these service standards are good enough for your customers, they are good enough for each other too. For example, how would the value of teamwork be strengthened if everyone anticipated each other's needs like they anticipated the customer's?

What kind of work environment could you foster with these principles in place? Imagine how quickly your customer loyalty and word-of-mouth marketing would increase if you insisted that everyone who represents your business is consistent with how they treat your customers?

When you have the guidelines established in which company culture can live and breathe through every decision and interaction, it keeps you focused as a Bombshell Business Woman and shows your employees how their jobs fit into the big picture, which keeps them interested and engaged.

Your mission statement, vision statement, core values, and service standards provide a clear focus for all while keeping your team humble and hungry. It creates that family environment in which your employees enjoy coming to work and dealing with the challenges they face each day.

Those cultural elements serve as a unifying standard. All decisions—whether goal setting, your employee conduct, how you handle recognition, how you handle discipline, how you handle customer feedback, or how you handle customer issues—are made with the culture serving as the defining measuring stick. Trust and loyalty, not only with your employees, but with your customers, are built through this common set of "family rules."

Take Action, Bombshell!

Visit www.thebombshellbusinesswoman.com for free, downloadable worksheets and resources.

1. *Create your mission statement. Clearly and concisely describe why your business exists.*

2. *Next, create your vision statement. Make it clear to the world what you aspire to achieve in the future.*

3. *Make a list of your company's core values. Explain each value briefly through a corresponding statement for each.*

4. *Decide which service standards are integral to your success, then describe them in a sentence or two.*

5. *Add all of these cultural basics to one document, and voila! You have a documented company culture.*

Congratulations on starting or reenergizing your existing business with a solid business foundation!

Eight

Developing Your Business Brand

Remember, in the Bombshell Business Dictionary we defined business as: *When an individual or group of individuals solve customer problems in exchange for money.*

But what makes that business competitive is its brand.

Your company brand is the second layer of the business success pyramid that rests on the foundation of your company culture. Stan Slap, author of *Under the Hood: How to Fire Up or Fine-Tune Your Employee Culture for Maximum Performance,* brilliantly points out, "You can't sell it outside if you can't sell it inside."[1]

When you are developing your brand, you want to dive even deeper into that problem and the people who have that problem so you can clearly communicate how you solve it uniquely from any other business offering similar solutions as yours.

For example, a fitness center exists to provide a location for its customers to exercise. Those customers may desire guidance, accountability, a sense of community, or state-of-the-art equipment. The "whys" behind their problems of not having a location to exercise are endless.

Perhaps they don't know how to safely exercise, or they had an injury and need more one-on-one attention to ensure their exercise is in line with their recovery plan. It could be that their doctor prescribed exercise in response to high cholesterol or high blood pressure, or to manage arthritis. It might be that they are trying to lose weight.

No matter why they are looking for a solution to that basic problem that categorizes your business, there is still a deeper reason they have the problem in the first place. Why is this potential fitness center customer trying to lose weight? What's the real problem at hand? It could be the need is to address physical or mental health challenges, to satisfy their vanity, to work on their self-esteem, to one day live out their dream of competing in a bodybuilding competition or running a marathon, or even to set a better example for their children. As you can see, the motivations can vary greatly.

So now we have a potential customer who wants:

1. A place to exercise . . .

2. So they can lose weight . . .

3. So they can achieve a specific goal that is unique to them.

But even knowing that much is not yet enough to develop a brand. Because that person also has an expectation of how they want to go about doing all of those things. So your company has to anticipate those expectations based on their demographics: age, income, education level, geographic location, lifestyle, and more. Knowing these things helps you attract that person to your business as a customer.

Don't worry, we'll get into how to identify these things and figure this out for your business in a later chapter. For now, I just want you to understand that even people who have similar problems have different expectations of service and experiences.

But wait . . . there's more!

Seriously, Amber? My head is spinning.

Stick with me!

Even if you know *all* of these things, there are still going to be companies similar to yours who attract customers who are similar to yours, so to get the right customers for your business, you must show them how you are different.

Your competition can be cheaper or more experienced, or have been in business longer. They can have more features, access to equipment you don't, or even stronger strategic alliances.

So to gain your share of the market, you must show how your company is different and how your culture produces a unique experience for your customers, leaving no room for competition. And that, Bombshell, is your brand.

If your culture is how you do business internally, your brand is what people believe about you externally. As you can see, one gives birth to the other, which is why establishing your company culture first is so critical.

NOW I LAY ME DOWN TO SLEEP

Loews Hotels is one of my all-time favorite clients because they vibrantly live out their company culture every day. They boast a diverse team of individuals who have a sincere desire to serve their guests and each other exceptionally. So as we look to this resort brand as an example, we can quickly identify the problem they solve: they provide lodging to people in their various markets who need a place to stay overnight.

However, so does La Quinta Inns. So why would someone

choose to stay at a Loews resort instead of a La Quinta Inns location?

The La Quinta Inns and Loews Hotels brands speak to two different types of customers completely. They offer different price points and appeal to different demographics. The way they solve the problem of lodging looks very different. Loews Hotels is a luxury brand, so it's not going to appeal to a La Quinta Inns customer, and La Quinta Inns is a limited-service hotel, so a Loews Hotels customer would not be attracted to it, even though they solve the same basic problem.

The Loews Hotels brand promise is, "We stay relevant to changing times and places to provide an experience that is authentically local and genuinely delivered, all so our guests can relax, explore, and flourish."[2]

Meanwhile, La Quinta Inns promises, "At La Quinta Inns, we're here to help both business and leisure travelers find their inner optimist. Your travel dollars go further with great rates and many free extras. Enjoy a free breakfast, comfy beds, and other amenities delivered with friendly service and a dose of humor."[3]

Yes, they have different price points, but they also display different brand personalities and offer expectations as to what is included in a room rate. Notice "relax, explore, and flourish" are the things that Loews Hotels wants its guests to do, while La Quinta Inns is talking about making your travel dollars go further with great rates and many free extras.

I know what you might be thinking: *Thanks, Captain Obvious, I never could have differentiated between a resort and a budget-friendly hotel.*

However, how clear are you making your brand right now? Can a person who has never stepped foot in your business or experienced doing business with you online tell the difference between what it's like to be your customer and the customer of a similar business who serves a different price point or demographic?

Yeah, I'm talking to you.

Do you currently and consistently portray how awesome it is to be your customer, or are you the best-kept secret in your industry or local community?

Mmm-hmm . . . moving on.

So I can ditch the Captain Obvious title and get your attention back on track, perhaps, let's invite a third option into this example. A lodging brand that has a price point similar to Loews Hotels and competes for a similar demographic is JW Marriott. Even when comparing apples to apples, it is clear each is still speaking to different customers when you examine their brand experiences.

JW Marriott is looking for guests who see themselves as accomplished. In fact, when speaking of their customers, Marriott says, "These accomplished professionals seek an environment of simple elegance where guests feel welcomed and free to be themselves. This is accomplished by orchestrating an experience that is expertly edited to leave only what is truly desired."[4]

Now that sounds a little more sophisticated or buttoned up when you compare it to Loews Hotels' promise to provide a place to "relax, explore, and flourish." So while these brands may look similar based on the amenities they offer or level of service one can expect, if you read each of their brand promises side by side, they're focusing on different outcomes for different types of guests.

Loews Hotels is focused on each hotel being uniquely local to its respective city. There are no cookie-cutter resorts in their portfolio. They want their guests to feel a part of their brand and a part of the particular city they are staying in. Their guests want the full immersion experience so they can "relax, explore, and flourish" as an ultimate goal.

JW Marriott, on the other hand, promotes a custom experience for people who value prominence and a desire for a service level that seems almost intuitively natural. They're probably not traveling with their dog like a Loews Hotels guest is allowed to. After all, they don't want any distractions since they greatly value their time as their most precious commodity. They are less likely to value "exploring" like a Loews Hotels guest might, and are more likely to want someone to think about what it is they need before even they know they need it.

JW Marriott is more of a timeless brand; Loews Hotels promises it is all about adapting to changing times and locations. One is not necessarily better than the other—both are amazingly high-touch, luxurious hotels. Yet, they are different in how they go about delivering excellence, creating different experiences for different types of customers.

Are there people who would be just as happy at a Loews resort as they would at JW Marriott? Absolutely. But all in all, these brands are created to instill a brand loyalty so that, say, a customer will choose to stay at a Loews Hotels if he's in a city where the Loews Hotels brand is an option.

As you can see, all three brands solve the same problem: a need for lodging. However, each brand offers a specific experience, attracting different types of guests, which in turn makes their marketing more targeted and their ability to meet the expectations of their guests more consistent.

YOUR BRAND PROMISE

Now that you have solid examples from some big players, it's time to create your own brand promise. A brand promise is, as you saw, the commitment to deliver on a company's promises to its audience. It is used to encourage its customer base to buy its product.

Your brand promise is basically saying, "Hey, this is what our business has to offer. Come invest your money and we'll solve your problems this particular way."

Warning: I do not want to see a vanilla-flavored brand statement. When it comes to branding, there is no room for average. I want you to show how you stand out so potential customers will experience your brand's marketing and immediately say, "Yes, that's for me," or, "No, that's not for me."

When it comes down to the nitty-gritty, answering only a couple of questions can actually create your brand promise. However, to be clear on those questions, it's important to explore several other questions to create the adjectives and descriptors that will add your unique business personality to your brand statement.

1. Describe your business in five words.

Is it luxurious? Are you about efficiency? Are you affordable? Are you custom or sustainable or holistic? Are you fair trade? High end?

There are so many different words you can use, and I want you to be very, very specific. And *don't use vanilla words.* Don't use words like *friendly.* If your business isn't friendly, then you need to go back to the drawing board, OK? *How* are you friendly? I want you to go deeper than those surface words that are easy to come up with. Bust out the thesaurus, ask your team members, ask your most loyal customers, and come up with five juicy words.

In my very first Bombshell Business Bootcamp Live, I had businesses from five counties in the greater Nashville area represented, and yet I also had several competing spas and salons who were literally within a few miles of each other. To show how unique each of their brands were, I shared each of their websites, logos, and other brand elements during my presentation and asked everyone in the room to start saying words that came to mind when each brand appeared. I wrote down the words as they were thrown out. At the end of the exercise, everybody in the room realized that while the competing spas might have been in the same business (meaning they solved the same problem in exchange for financial compensation), their brands were so completely different it was hard to truly consider each one competition.

Let me emphasize that point. When your brand shows just how unique your customer experience is, you eliminate competition because your customers refuse to have an experience that is different from yours.

Do you know any Apple computer fanatics?

I rest my case.

2. What do your customers say about you to their friends?

This is a really big deal. Most people have about fifteen people in their life that they talk to regularly every single week. They talk about what seems to them like mundane life happenings: where they went, what they bought, what they ate, etc. In the context of your customer's everyday life, what is she offhandedly saying about your brand to those fifteen people? Now think about how each of those people have fifteen people in their life, and so on, and you can see how one "off-brand" experience can quickly spread like wildfire. Then add social media and the bad experience just went nuclear. Or, if it was a positive experience, the same type of momentum can attract a slew of new customers. But it starts with being aware of what is being said in the first place.

3. What do you do?

Oh, wait. That's not so simple to answer, is it? But that's

only because you are overcomplicating it. Ever ask a person at a networking event, "What is it that you do?"

Then you stand and wait while it takes them, oh, about ninety minutes to explain while you are eyeballing the charcuterie board on the buffet table, all the while waiting for your chance to escape and find solace in cured meats and gourmet cheeses.

So, for the purpose of this exercise, keep it very simple. I'm not asking you to come up with an elevator pitch here.

"I cut, color, and style hair."

"I offer spa services."

"I sell upscale homes."

"I provide family law services."

"I design websites for small businesses."

4. Who do you do it for?

Again, dial this in; don't be general. Do you work with recently divorced women? Do you work with families who are going from their current home to their dream home? Do you work with single moms? I want you to be as specific as possible.

The people I work with one on one are generally high-end service providers who have a team of some sort, whether they are full-time employees or vendors they routinely contract with. If I dial it in even more, it's probably going to be someone in the spa or salon industry simply because their needs and problems are most like my large hospitality clients, and I can easily use the same language and strategies.

Do I also serve lawyers, real estate agents, interior designers, fitness professionals, consultants, artists, wellness practitioners, retail outfits, and more? Absolutely.

Yet it would take a long time, a considerable amount of money, and more energy than I have to go after all those audiences. So while I stay targeted in my messaging to one audience, countless other industry professionals simply see this: "Oh, Amber helps premium brand service providers." They find me, anyway.

I'm not kicking anybody out of the club; I'm really just focusing my message and then leaving the door open for anybody else who happens to be drawn to that message as well. It's way too hard to be everything to everybody. However, when you are clear about who you serve, your messaging and targeting becomes much easier, and others with similar attributes and problems will see how they fit in your brand experience.

5. Now that you have declared what you do and who do you do it for, explain how you do it *uniquely*.

OK, all aboard the struggle bus! This is where most Bombshells hit a brick wall. In fairness, it is difficult to describe without understanding how you fit in the marketplace. However, once you start checking out your competition and compare your answers to questions number one and two of this exercise to the answers that would likely fit your competitors, you begin to see how you are, in fact, different.

You can't be scared of your competition or have a sense of rivalry. A high tide raises all ships. Just dial in on who it is you're going after as a customer, and then let go of any unhealthy feelings toward your competition.

6. List some of the "Wow!" moments you've had with your customers or employees, then circle the words that describe the feelings everyone experienced.

I want you to come up with some adjectives that describe the soul of your business. How do you make your customers feel when they interact with you? JW Marriott and Loews Hotels both acknowledge how they want guests to feel when they're doing business with them, and you should be that confident too.

7. What do you want to be known for?

Again, this seems to be an easy question, but it is hard to dial it in, especially if you are multipassionate. Let me return to using myself as an example. I am known for my "velvet machete." My audience knows I'm going to shoot them straight and keep it real, but they also know it comes from a place of love and is accompanied by an interest in their ultimate success and happiness. I'm not for everyone, and that's a good thing!

Maybe you're the edgy salon in a small town, like Jennie Walpole's Asante Masters at the Mill, which is near me. Or perhaps you are the "one-stop shop for all things beauty," like Necole Bell's Beauty Boutique, which offers salon and spa services as well as higher-end clothing their customers would otherwise have to drive at least thirty miles to find. Or perhaps you are known for a more "holistic, integrated wellness" approach like Julie Miller-Wilson and Heather Hull's Body Kneads, Etc., a full-service day spa that focuses on total wellness. (It has done well enough that it will soon be expanding to a larger location and will include fitness and even nutrition services.)

All three of these women-owned businesses are within a ten-minute drive from my house in Lebanon, Tennessee, and they each have services that overlap and compete. At the same time, each brand is clearly known for their distinct experiences, so they tend to attract different clientele. By focusing on what they want to be known for, they make deciding on their offerings, marketing, and promotions, as well as their customer experience, much easier.

Oh, and I've witnessed these Bombshells, outside the

context of my program or consulting, help each other and encourage one another behind the scenes. It's incredible to see powerful, confident women elevate even their own competition when so many expect to view a cat fight or at least tearing one another other down.

That's the power of being a Bombshell: you can be a bold, brave, and unwaveringly confident fempreneur. You get to do business on a different level!

OK, now let's take all of your responses from that exercise and get down to brass tacks: your brand promise.

Here's the formula: List your company name, the problems you solve, how you solve them uniquely, and for who.

Now, that's the meat of it, but remember, you answered all those other questions to get the feelings, emotions, and descriptors you'll need to complete the important statement at the end of this chapter.

It doesn't have to be long. In fact, you don't want it to be wordy. Unlike your Business Mojo, this is something you do want to share with your customers and potential customers. It's something you want your employees to genuinely be able to understand and digest so they can deliver that very brand experience to your customers.

Take Action, Bombshell!

Visit www.thebombshellbusinesswoman.com for free, downloadable worksheets and resources.

1. *Complete the exercises within this chapter.*

2. *Using the words that express the essence of your brand, complete the following formula to come up with your brand promise:*

Your company name

solves this problem

uniquely this way

for these specific people.

Nine

Understanding Your Personal Brand

Right now Nashville's definitely an "it" city with a hot restaurant scene. The competition is fierce, and if I ate at a new restaurant for breakfast, lunch, and dinner for months, I wouldn't come close to getting caught up on all of the great food.

However, my husband and I have one restaurant, Urban Grub, that is in our handful of go-tos, simply because it is consistently good and moderately priced for everyday dining. Wilson, our favorite server there, was fun and knew what you wanted to eat or drink just by looking at you. In fact, we would often come in and Wilson would say, "I've got your meal figured out. You don't need to order"—and then walk away. We didn't mind because we knew Wilson's selections would far exceed what we might come up with ourselves. From our first visit on, no one ever waited on our table except Wilson.

Then Wilson left the restaurant.

Needless to say, I was distraught. (Hey, I'm a foodie. This is serious business here.) Yet, we returned consistently because the food, ambience, and rest of the team were still sure things.

One evening in the post-Wilson era, we were sitting at our little table, drinking our wine and enjoying our deliciously golden tapioca popovers with honey butter as we waited on our appetizers. We looked over at another table and saw that their server was super animated and sported a serious hipster beard. He was commanding a presence in the room despite being three or four tables away and having nothing to do with our experience that evening.

I looked over at my husband. "Oh, my gosh. It's Wilson in training."

"I was just about to say that," he affirmed.

It just so happened that Wilson-to-be brought our food to our table, which we were happy about since we planned to meet him before we left.

He greeted us. "Hey, guys. My name's James. Hope you enjoy this, and I hope you all are having a very nice evening tonight at Urban Grub."

We were, again, quite impressed. Of course, because I work in branding every day and know how important it is for career servers to build up a regular clientele, I said, "Man, he's so freakin' smart. He told us his name."

We were suddenly very interested in this James fellow.

When he walked by our table again, my husband stopped him to properly introduce ourselves, and we told him we would ask for him the next time we were in. He graciously thanked us and said he would look forward to it.

We continued to watch James.

He was serving a twelve-top table of millennial couples celebrating a special occasion, and he began describing one of the specials: "All right, gang. This dish is going to be sweet and tangy."

Then he holds up his hand and starts counting off his fingers one by one with each description. "Y'all got your sweet, you got your tangy, you got your salty."

He understood the energy of the group and sucked them into the menu. He used body language and spoke in a way familiar and friendly with each of them, as if they had been friends for years.

Later we got up to leave quietly and say good-bye to James while trying not to interrupt the twelve-top's evening.

"Hey, thanks for coming in, Geoff and Amber," he responded. "I'll see you guys soon."

He remembered our names!

Now, there was nothing wrong with our server. She was lovely. She was very sweet, she handled us well, she took care of our every need. But we just happen to love a highly engaged, big personality, one who adores selling whatever it is the chef created. We tend to want to have that kind of fun, interactive, high-fiving, laughing, talking-about-the-food, joking-around experience. Obviously, James is a great fit for us and the type of evening we like.

By expressing his personal brand, we, the customers, were able to say, "That's our kind of server. We want to do business with him."

So, let's go back to the Business Success Pyramid and let me tell you how this story fits in.

Urban Grub obviously has a great culture because there is consistency with its employees, the food, and simply how they do business all around. They have these foundations strongly in place.

Then, of course, the restaurant has its brand, meaning what their customers and potential customers believe about the restaurant. Because it has a strong internal culture, their customer experience, and therefore brand reputation, nicely rests on that, as you can see in the pyramid presented earlier in the book.

Yet, every person in that company has their own personal brand. The executive chef's reputation rests in carefully crafted foods, from grinding his own iconic smoked gouda grits to the team curing their own charcuterie meats. The super friendly general manager makes everyone feel like a regular, and he handles problems in a way that makes you forget there was even a problem to begin with. Then you have James and everyone else working there, from the hostess to the bartender to the guy who shucks your oysters at brunch.

They all have their own personal brands in addition to the Urban Grub brand, and I guarantee you that James leveraging his personal brand in support of the Urban Grub brand makes Urban Grub a lot more money.

Why? Because he can upsell like a boss. He gets into his food descriptions, inviting diners into the story of the food. Customers likely trust his expertise so much that they select a more expensive glass of wine, order dessert that they weren't planning on getting, and splurge on the special he made irresistible through his careful illustration. So he's obviously making more money in food sales and, also, in his personal tips.

Now, that being said, James is not for everyone. If you don't want a more boisterous server and you prefer a low-key person, James would not be the best server for you.

In fact, James would probably immediately turn you off, and that's an OK thing. He cannot operate in his most natural way if his dinner service is full of nonfoodies. That's not fun for him, and it's not fun for the true foodies who are waiting for his energy to restore itself for them (this, possibly, after he's had to dull down for a table, where he's not making as much money on top of everything else).

You can't be "it" for everyone. In fact, if you try to please everyone, you will please no one, especially yourself.

To perform at his best and be his most influential, it is best for James to build up a solid group of regulars who specifically ask for him. Then he knows each table will be easier to wait on because he will know their preferences and personalities, and he will know that his tips will be consistent, which is not always the case for a server who waits on whoever gets seated in his or her section.

This group of regulars is going to be a subsection of Urban Grub's client base that is attracted to James's personal brand.

While everyone in your business should be aware of their superpowers so they can best serve customers and fellow team members, it's critical if you're a day spa owner full of competing practitioners, a salon owner with several stylists, a law firm with associates, a fitness center with trainers—or any business where many people offer the same service.

You've got to get your team to not only understand your company brand, but also to understand their personal brand.

When I consult with businesses like these, I love asking individuals in the group, "Why would I hire you and not her?" Then, I point to a colleague who is sitting right next to the person I'm addressing. You should see their faces. It jars them. They don't want to act like they're competing with their friends at work.

That's why I love teaching the concept of personal branding, because only then do you realize if your personal brand is strong enough; it eliminates competition all together. With a strong personal brand, you become the only option in the eyes of your ideal customer.

Think James at the Urban Grub.

No other server even has the chance to compete for our tips

since James eliminated his competition simply by being himself, fully, and naturally creating an experience my husband and I never want to do without when we visit that restaurant.

WHAT A PERSONAL BRAND IS AND WHAT YOUR PERSONAL BRAND IS *NOT*

Jeff Bezos, the founder of Amazon, is credited with saying, "Your personal brand is what people say about you when you're not in the room."[1]

Simmer on that for a second.

So what *are* people saying about you when you're not in the room?

If you are unsure or dissatisfied with the answer to that question, allow me to guide you through changing that story.

Your personal brand is a snapshot of who you authentically are as an individual and what you uniquely offer the world. It helps people quickly identify with you, and it enables you to attract the right people to your life. It provides an immediate perception that puts you top-of-mind for specific opportunities others may come across.

It's going to increase people contacting you to say, "Hey, I thought about you for this," or, "I recommended you to a friend," or even, "You have to meet this other business owner. You two would totally click!"

That said, your personal brand is not the promotion of an idea of who you are or even who you want to become. It's not trying to be what you want others to think you are. It's not a personal public relations campaign. You cannot create a personal brand that is *not who you are at the gut level.* You can try to convince people you are someone God did not design you to be. But it's not going to work because it's too much work—too draining—to keep up the facade. Not to mention people will be turned off when you are faking it—and you will lose, instead of build, trust.

Get on board with brand *you.*

Much like how a company brand is an outward, public-facing reflection of an internal company culture, a personal brand is the outward, public-facing reflection of your gifts, talents, life philosophies, personal values, and the lens through which you see the world.

HOW TO DEVELOP YOUR PERSONAL BRAND

To develop your personal brand, you first need to gain clarity on how you see yourself. Then you need to understand how other people see you and know what they are saying about you "when you're not in the room." Equipped with this knowledge, you will be able to identify what gaps you need to close between who you are and how you are perceived. Then you can create a personal brand statement you can use to stay focused on pursuing opportunities and relationships that keep you in your wheelhouse, allowing you to fast-track your success and eliminate competition.

Of course, if there are no gaps, then rock on with your bad self. You can just focus on what parts of your brand you can amplify to increase your visibility or your level of attraction for people and opportunities that fit the best for you.

Going through this process can be a little scary, or it can be crazy fun, depending on your personality. Most Bombshells enjoy this process because they're so focused on their business, employees, and families that it's a special treat to turn the focus on themselves.

Just imagine what it will be like to go inward and start looking at who you are and what you want to be known for as an individual. It's going to be one of the most important exercises you can complete to enjoy life on your terms.

Are you ready? Grab your favorite journal and let's do this!

1. What is your life's mission or purpose? Meaning, how do you uniquely fit in the world and contribute in a meaningful way?

2. What are your top three to five values? Your values are the lens through which you see the world, and they're an indicator of what's most important to you. Most of your decisions are filtered through these personal standards.

3. What are three to five words you use to describe your personality? If you could pick five words and only five words, what would they be? These words are incredibly telling of how you want people to see you if you're really being true to who you are.

4. What are your core strengths? What are the things you've always been inherently good at? Are you that person everybody comes to talk with about their problems? Are you a natural leader? Have you consistently been skilled at organizing? Write down the things that come easily to you.

Bombshell Case Study

Bombshell Angela Korman is a math whiz. Her career history includes keeping the books and excelling as an accountant extraordinaire for the businesses who employ her. Her accounting degree did not come easily as an adult returning student and mom to Eleanor, but her ability to analyze a business's finances did.

Through a series of serendipitous events, Angela fell in love with executive chef Kevin Korman. They had a magical wedding, welcomed their baby, Roselyn, and continued to plan a future for their blended family.

Together, they launched Roselie Dining and Seafood Bar, an upscale, yet child friendly, restaurant in Florida's South Walton Beach area; it's named after Eleanor and Roselyn. With Kevin's vast culinary and restaurant experience and Angela's business operations and human resource experience, they are now proud entrepreneurs whose restaurant has been featured on national television and in print publications.

From accountant to restaurateur, Angela leveraged her natural gifts in a way even she never expected.

5. What are you the "go to" person for in helping others? Are you the person who can fix computer problems? Do you always know the right thing to say in a difficult situation? Are you the numbers girl, or are you the hostess with the mostess? When people come to you and they're like, "Hey, I need help, and of course I'd come to you." What is that thing you do to bring this out?

6. What role do you fill in your friend group? Remember the TV sitcom *The Golden Girls?* Each of the roommates in that series had a distinct character: Dorothy was the serious, stoic one who kept the group on track. Blanche was the sultry one who kept things interesting. Rose was funny, playful, and naive, the one who brought everyone together. Then Sophia was the spitfire, "tell-it-like-it-is" senior of the group; she provided both the needed comic relief and a kick in the pants for all the roommates.

If you and your friends were the cast of a TV show, what would your character be known for?

7. What impact have you had on organizations you have

worked for, or what impact do you have within your own organization? Whether you have always owned your business, or were an employee, how have you moved the needle in support of where that business was trying to go?

For example, I have been consistently hired throughout my career to next-level a position or a department. Looking at my career history, you can see I was hired to either create a position or take an existing position to a new level of creativity while using documented, consistent processes.

I'm an innovator, and I'm passionate. When you combine those two things, it is natural to not only create out-of-the-box, exciting solutions that change the way of doing business, it is equally important to get the buy-in of others who are, or eventually will be, impacted by the change.

Change is hard. I don't know anybody who is like, "Oh, I just love change! It's super comfortable."

So, I have been known for moving through change and doing it with consensus along the journey, and bringing a new level of excellence as well. It's no surprise I continue to do that and teach other businesses how to do the same through my consulting and speaking.

Now I go back to my question: What is it you've consistently done over your career that stands the test of time?

8. What are a few accomplishments you're proud of?

Bombshell Case Study

Bombshell Deidre DeFelice has been the director of operations for the Blowout Co., a dry bar with locations in Nashville and Chattanooga, Tennessee, since the opening of its first plush storefront. Deidre created the menu of services, as well as the processes stylists use to give consistent and efficient blowouts for their customers, saving time on training and ultimately creating a fast and affordable, yet indulgent, experience. Deidre keeps her team focused on being "day-makers" every time they step behind the chair.

After seeing the success her experience and processes created, Deidre realized she wanted to empower even more stylists to be day-makers as well. The end experience of a happy woman who feels beautiful and pampered, even just for a day, is what she is most proud of, what her personal brand exudes. Now, with the blessing of Blowout Co. ownership, Deidre goes to noncompeting markets to teach the art and science of the perfect blowout, in its many styles and forms, through her side hustle, The Blowout Academy.

9. What do people say about you when describing you to people who don't know you? Yep, we're at the "What do people say about you when you're not in the room?" question. After reviewing what you believe about yourself, it's important to start recognizing the gaps between who you know you are and how you are perceived.

For example, I worked with a capable, experienced, and engaged executive within a Fortune 500 healthcare company. With no history of poor performance reviews, this leader struggled with getting her work done every day, not to mention garnering respect from peers and superiors. Her team was frustrated for her and their department, and she was at her wit's end. Through tears, she explained how horrified she was that she had a poor annual review for the first time in her career.

After experiencing how intelligent and heartfelt this woman was, I knew there had to be a disconnect in her personal brand. Together we explored what people were saying about her when she was not in the room, and we realized they saw her as a country girl, one who rambled in meetings and did not always prioritize the interest of the company's goals.

While it was painful to recognize, because those assumptions couldn't have been further from the truth, it was imperative to address them to craft a plan to rebuild her personal brand through trust. If she wanted to once again become the influential businesswoman she was accustomed to being known as throughout her career, it was time to address the truth and take action to overcome the disparity.

Her months and months of commitment in working with me to craft her personal brand, and her extreme intention in how she communicated and engaged with others, paid off. This femfessional (female professional) was recognized in an important meeting as one of the most important key influencers in her region. On top of everything, she found herself listening to glowing praise in her next annual review.

With this powerful transformation as an example, consider how even small improvements can help you advance your business and your life.

PULLING IT ALL TOGETHER

Having answered these nine questions, let's talk about the strengths or personality attributes you need to better promote yourself so *who you are* aligns with *how people see you*.

I use the term *promote* gingerly here, because it's not like you are going to walk into a room and say, "Hi, I'm Susie, and I'm awesome at organizing and interpersonal communication."

What I mean by promote is I want you to exude the strengths and personality attributes you identified through this chapter. Put yourself in positions where you can shine in those areas, find opportunities to showcase those strengths through helping people problem-solve, storytelling in networking situations, or by actually doing these things in a professional setting.

Still struggling? Here are a few more questions to ask yourself to define the gap.

- What do you need to highlight to better showcase what your closest friends and family already know about you?

- What aren't people dialing in on quickly that is keeping you from positioning yourself for success?

- What strengths do others need to be aware of to see you as an authority who attracts and engages the people you need to have in your life to achieve your goals? (Because, remember, it's not just about business. If you aren't attracting the right people in general—your friend group, the right life partner, etc.—it is going to be more challenging to elevate yourself to what you are ultimately capable of.)

Just as you defined what made your business unique when you created your business brand, now you must decide how can you differentiate yourself from others. What is your personal competitive advantage? I want you to identify how you stand out within your business or among your industry peers.

Take Action, Bombshell!

Visit www.thebombshellbusinesswoman.com for free, downloadable worksheets and resources.

1. *Complete the questions in this chapter.*

2. *Ask your friends, peers, employees, and colleagues, "What is it that I can do better than anybody else?"*

3. *Make a list of common themes you receive in your feedback.*

4. *Identify whether you see yourself the way other people see you.*

5. *If you don't, then bridge that gap by being more intentional in showing who you really are in every opportunity you can.*

6. *If you do, congrats! Now live that personal brand loudly and continue to expand your reach and influence!*

Bonus points: Take each of your team members through this exercise so they can define and exude their own "Wow!" factors as well.

Ten

Creating a Bombshell Basic Business Plan

Maybe you want to scale your business, but you've never put a plan together and you've been flying by the seat of your pants. Or maybe you are just starting out and want a solid road map. Either way, I'm going to walk you through writing a basic, nonthreatening business plan.

I know this is a touchy topic in the land of entrepreneurs.

As much as I'm a "Screw it—just do it" advocate, I like to use that phrase more in situations where I am making a calculated risk. If my gut is telling me to do it, I'm going to go for it. However, aimlessly running your business is not going to net you the same results as being aware of what your current reality is, and having a plan for where you are going. So let's go on a mental road trip together.

You're in Texas and you want to drive to South Carolina. You Google Map it, decide how much gas you need, what stops you might want to take along the way, and ensure your vehicle is roadworthy, right? You have a plan. That doesn't mean you can't pull off the main highway because you want to explore something you didn't know about, and maybe you can take a back road somewhere along the way to your destination.

But a plan is still extremely useful; it helps you keep moving toward your destination without driving all over the country to get from Texas to South Carolina. You won't backtrack, you won't waste money on gas or car repairs that you didn't count on, and you won't likely get lost because you went too far off the route you planned to take. And, equally important, the people in the car you are driving toward your destination are a lot less likely to get cranky or travel-weary because you're driving them all over the place aimlessly. They will trust you to get there without asking "are we there, yet?" a zillion times.

A plan is not putting you in a box and forcing you to stay there. A plan is a guide to keep you on course, efficient, and safe. Simple as that.

William B. Gartner, Clemson University entrepreneurship professor, and his colleagues looked at data from the Panal Study of Entrepreneurial Dynamics. This study reflected eight hundred people who were starting a business. What the study discovered is you're two and a half times more likely to get into business with a solid plan versus trying to do so without such a template.[1]

What if you are trying to next-level? Wouldn't a plan give you the same amount of confidence and direction to do that as it would a new business?

Use the Bombshell Basic Business Plan—offered in this chapter—to guide you in building a clear path for your business's future. Please know these are not all-inclusive, and you can always add information and research how to create a full-fledged business plan using the resources at the end of this chapter.

You will need more financial data and projections, more market analysis, and more day-to-day operational verbiage if you are creating a document for funding or for tax authorities in the US.

Those circumstances aside, this quick Bombshell Business Basic Business Plan is enough to get you moving in a positive direction with focus, clarity, and intention. The key message I intend here is that this process is not meant to overwhelm you. A business plan is simply a snapshot of where "here" is for your business and where you want to go.

Follow these steps to create a Bombshell Business Basic Business Plan of your own.

IDENTIFY YOUR MANAGEMENT TEAM

- Who is in your leadership team?
- What are their roles?
- Are there plans to fill their positions if they move on? (This is called succession planning.)
- If you do not have a team, what roles would you fill if money were no object? (This will help you prioritize creating future positions.)

CREATE YOUR SMART GOALS

- Specific: target a specific area for improvement.
- Measurable: quantify or at least suggest an indicator of progress.
- Assignable: specify who will do it.
- Realistic: state what results can realistically be achieved given available resources.
- Time-related: have deadlines for your goals.

Note: Be certain you have financial goals that are presented in "x to y by when" format and can be broken down into smaller mini goals (e.g. "Grow consulting gross revenue from $34,000 annually to $42,0000 annually by December 15, 20__"). Then break down what that revenue growth will look like by month or quarter, understanding you may wish to sandbag one month that is seasonally more profitable over another, or you may strive for steady, equal growth for each mini checkpoint.

CREATE A SWOT ANALYSIS (STRENGTHS, WEAKNESSES, OPPORTUNITIES, THREATS)

Strengths
- What is your competitive advantage?
- What do you do really well?
- What resources exceptionally help your operation?
- What are you most proud of?
- Who on your team are superstars, and why?
- What are your personal strengths that impact your business?

Weaknesses
- Where do you lag in your market space?
- What tools or resources do you not have and need or want?
- What roles do you need to fill, but haven't or can't?
- Who on your team keeps you from performing at your best?

Opportunities
- What has shifted in the market that opens a door for your growth?

- What new markets might be developing that you can take advantage of?

- What shifts in materials or vendor availability can you leverage to your advantage?

Threats (Areas of Concern)

- What makes you lose sleep at night?

- What would you immediately change if you could to improve your business?

- Who are your chief competitors?

- Who else has a market share in your space?

- What are each of their strengths?

- What are each of their weaknesses?

Create Goals for Professional Services to Help You Grow

- What type of help do you think you specifically need (legal, financial, HR, leadership coaching, real estate, etc.)?

- What problems do you need solutions for to help you resolve things?

- What growth would you like guidance in from an advisor?

* * * * * * *

After mapping out these key areas for your business, you'll be able to remain more focused, more effectively delegate work, project future earnings and expenses, and just overall feel like you've got your poop in a group.

Now see? That wasn't so bad. Congratulations on creating a plan!

Take Action, Bombshell!

Visit www.thebombshellbusinesswoman.com for free,
downloadable worksheets and resources.

1. Download and complete the Bombshell Basic Business Plan found online in the free resources mentioned above.

2. Consider using more comprehensive business plan templates by visiting the US Small Business Administration Business Plan Builder (https://www.sba.gov/tools/business-plan/1) or the SCORE Business Plan Builder (https://www.score.org/content/business-plan-resources).

Eleven

The Glamour Goals Process

Good gracious almighty, Amber. You have a name for everything, don't you?

Yes, and I have your attention with my consistent branding, don't I? Stick with me, kid. You'll learn a few things (said in my best old mobster movie voice).

You see, once you have a Bombshell Basic Business Plan you should set goals to ensure its success.

Now, what the heck are Glamour Goals?

Let's start by defining glamour:

glam·our (noun) *the attractive or exciting quality that makes certain people or things seem appealing or special.*[1]

Thinking back, how appealing or special have your goals in the past truly been?

Most of the time we don't meet our goals because we don't have a big enough "why" behind them, or because we aren't sure how to back into bigger goals with realistic, actionable plans.

So it's no wonder they aren't attractive, nor are they exciting to us.

Since planning isn't the sexy part of doing business, I'm here to glam it up and make it fun. Throughout this chapter you will learn how to ensure your annual business goals are truly bold, desirable, and destined to reach success. You will walk through the step-by-step process I take my clients through so you can implement your new knowledge into your unique business immediately.

Years ago, I was so fortunate to experience the great Zig Ziglar when he came to Nashville. A master motivator, he said in his book *See You at the Top*, "I don't care how much power, brilliance, or energy you have, if you don't harness it and focus it on a specific target, and hold it there, you're never going to accomplish as much as your ability warrants."[2]

So that's what creating Glamour Goals is all about: focusing that power, brilliance, and energy on a target. You are not creating a handful of things we hope to accomplish. No, Bombshell, you will laser in on just a few Glamour Goals so you can finally accomplish what you are capable of.

Whether you are at the beginning of your fiscal year or near the end, go through this seven-step process. Then, when the new year approaches, you will be an old pro at setting Glamour Goals.

STEP 1: MAP OUT EVERY PART OF YOUR LIFE BY MONTH

The first step in the Glamour Goals process is annual planning. Each year, map out every part of your life that you can think of.

That means before you do anything or start to consider what you might want to accomplish, you need to map out every part of your life, by each month, that you are already aware of.

This will help you be realistic about your time, energy, and resources when mapping out your action plan. Simply divide a sheet of paper into whatever number of months are left in your fiscal year, and note underneath each month what obligations you have for that month.

Be sure to include:

- Personal celebrations (holidays, birthdays, anniversaries, etc., that you will be significantly involved in)

- School-related dates for kids or yourself (breaks, start-end dates, exams, etc.)

- Travel (vacations, work-related, conventions, weddings, etc.)

Note naturally busy seasons at work or annual product launches, events, or other ongoing business-related dates that are regularly scheduled or already in the works.

Hang on to this paper! We'll come back to it in a future step in the Glamour Goal process!

Track everything—and I mean *everything*—prior to creating your goals because goals have deadlines, and those deadlines require a lot of prework on the road to accomplishing them.

When I go through this process with my one-on-one clients, they are astonished at how much they are already committed to. Being aware of how busy each month or even each part of the month is to begin with will help you chart your goals and deadlines in a way that is realistic and won't leave you feeling overwhelmed and frustrated. (After all, frowning causes wrinkles, and we can't have that now, can we?)

So go ahead, pull out all your calendars. Go to your kids'

schools' websites, check your community calendars, look at your past years' calendars for dates you might have forgotten about this year, and call your mama. (She always knows what you're overlooking, right?) Gather all of your goods, and then move on to the next step.

STEP 2: IDENTIFY GLAMOUR GOALS

Now that you've laid out every detail you're aware of for the rest of your fiscal year, let's start talking about your actual Glamour Goals.

Identify the three to five things you must accomplish in order to move closer to who you want to become professionally and personally.

Examples could include goals like: increase revenue by 13 percent, increase customer satisfaction by 10 percent, hire and retain two new employees, launch a new product, get a certification, finish writing your book, etc.

Notice I asked you who you want to become. If, for example, you increased your revenue by 13 percent over last year, is it so you can become a better provider? Or is it so you can one day enjoy enough income to take luxury vacations? Do you wish to become a philanthropist and spread your money all over the world among charities you adore? Seriously, picture yourself in the future . . . what does that 13 percent increase this year mean to your future self? Now that you have that in mind, I want you to think more immediately on the steps you need to take—now—to get there.

Also, notice I asked for *only* three to five goals.

I understand there's a lot you want to accomplish in the coming year. However, the greats will tell you to focus your efforts on what truly matters. Everything else is a distraction from truly committing to getting the massively important stuff done.

It's been said that Warren Buffet advised an employee to write down twenty-five things he wanted to accomplish. Then, Buffet instructed the employee to circle the top five most important things on the list. From there he adamantly insisted the other twenty things be forgotten about until the top five goals were accomplished.

I'm going to squeeze you even harder than that. I challenge you to truly narrow it down to three. Can you do that? Can you focus that intensely on what matters in your business more than anything else?

OK. Perfect. Now, stick with me . . .

Why do each of these Glamour Goals matter *this year*? What makes them glamorous? Remember, the definition of glamour is the attractive or exciting quality that makes certain people or things seem appealing or special.

If you increase revenue by 13 percent, could you hire an assistant, eliminate bringing work home at night, and spend more time with your family and friends? Yes? That sounds a lot more compelling than a number with a percentage sign after it on profit and loss sheet!

So now, simply list each goal, and then explain its glamour factor. In other words, you will not only document your super, ultra, amazingly important goals. You will also put into words what makes them appealing or special so you can revisit them when the going gets tough—or when the tough gets distracted by shiny object syndrome!

STEP 3: TEST YOUR GLAMOUR GOALS

Before we chisel these Glamour Goals into stone, you want to do both a gut check and a reality check to ensure they are in alignment with your company culture and can stand up against the inevitable trials that could possibly derail them.

First, let's do a gut check: Do your three Glamour Goals align with your company's mission, vision, and values?

If yes, carry on. If no, go back to the drawing board!

Now it's time for a reality check: What are possible obstacles that could get in the way of achieving those goals? Could it be employee turnover? Uncertain revenue cycles? A sick parent? Seasonal depression? Being distracted by other opportunities? Overcommitting in the volunteer area? What are those obstacles for you? List at least one challenge you can foresee arising for every goal you have listed. This is a great team exercise, by the way, so consider asking for feedback from your employees.

Now, here's where the important part comes in! What are solutions to those possible obstacles? I want you to triple down on every obstacle and list three solutions to each problem you listed. This will ensure that when a crisis strikes you already have ways to overcome your challenge all mapped out, all while you remain in a cool, calm frame of mind!

To recap step three:

- Gut-check each of your Glamour Goals.

- Do a reality check on each of your Glamour Goals.

- Come up with one potential obstacle you might face for each Glamour Goal.

- Create three solutions to each potential obstacle you identify.

Now, for the mathematically challenged among us, that means you have three Glamour Goals, three potential obstacles, and *nine* solutions.

Why so many solutions? Go back and read my story in

chapters two and three. Life comes at you hard. Why wait like a sitting duck when you can be proactive?

Don't be tempted to skip this step of the Glamour Goals process. It's very important. Your future self will thank you for setting her up for success by being a future problem solver!

STEP 4: CREATE MINI GOALS FOR EACH GLAMOUR GOAL

It's not enough to set a goal. Antoine de Saint-Exupéry famously said, "A goal without a plan is just a wish."[3]

That's why you have to back into your due dates for *each* of your Glamour Goals, then create mini goals with progressive timelines to get you there.

Let's use a more personal example to illustrate how this works: if you want to lose twenty pounds in the coming year, then you know you obviously can't just wake up at the first of December and start gunning it to your leaner self. That's ridiculous, right?

Well, then why risk doing that with your business goals? You simply can't procrastinate. So realistically, if you want to lose twenty pounds in the next year as a personal Glamour Goal, you might create mini goals such as: 1) hire a personal trainer by January 7; 2) test body fat percentage on the 30th of every month; 3) take a healthy eating cooking class by March; 4) join a volleyball league by June. And you might have a fail-safe, in case you are still struggling, that if you don't have control of your nutrition by July, you might have a mini goal of researching and selecting a health coach to help carry your efforts out through the remainder of the year.

After exploring your mini goals, how much more confident are you in your ability to achieve your twenty-pound Glamour Goal?

Now it's time to tie it all together.

First, pull back out your Annual Planning from step one. Next, compare your preliminary mini goal timelines to your Annual Planning calendar. Can you realistically accomplish your mini goals in support of your Glamour Goals with everything that is naturally going on in each season? Do you need to rethink some of your timelines to better set yourself up for success? Or perhaps you should accelerate a timeline for one of your goals when you determine you have a slower period in your life that could be used for these higher-level goals?

Once you've cleared your timelines against the reality of your calendar and life, assign each mini goal to you, a team member, or a business or strategic partner, then note any other helpful information you may need to document along the way.

Bombshell Quick Tips

- Each mini goal should show an actionable change by a specific date.

- Once you are certain your plan is as rock solid as it can be, create a spreadsheet of all your Glamour Goals and the time-bound mini goals that support them. You can keep it organized by each Glamour Goal or you can sort by date for one chronological master plan.

- Either way, you will have your master plan in one place, which we will discuss in the next step.

Look over every step twice and then give it a third read to be sure every step you need to take toward your Glamour Goals are listed as mini goals. If you don't like using spreadsheets, don't let that stop you. Get out a piece of paper and a pen, if that is your thing, but do create a timeline so you can have a master plan for success.

STEP 5: CREATE (AND POST) A GLAMOUR GOALS VISION AND PROGRESS BOARD

To keep the enthusiasm of your team (or simply you) focused and excited about your Glamour Goals for the entire year, the next step in the process is to create a vision and progress board to track your success.

If you're one who likes to stay digitally organized, then keep a spreadsheet, as mentioned, on your Google Drive or other shareable location so you can share it with others who are helping you achieve your goals.

Yet, importantly, put a visually appealing version of your vision and progress board in your office to keep you focused. How? I'm so glad you asked!

If your Glamour Goals are truly worth pursuing, if you want your entire team to see what they're contributing to day to day, if you want to keep an even scoreboard where *both* wins are accounted for and losses addressed, then create a fun, compelling vision and progress board and post it in a highly visible area.

First, you want to post visuals at the top of your board that remind you of your Glamour Goals to begin with. Want to increase your revenue? How about posting a picture of a rapper with money "raining" all around him? Want to improve customer service? Add a photo of a game show contestant running excitedly down the studio aisle. Have fun with this!

The bottom half of your vision and progress board should show the "progress" part of that equation. Create a theme for the year's Glamour Goals that will motivate you and your team to focus on the plan while making it entertaining. Life's too short to be all serious all the time.

If you have a team, I encourage you to include them when brainstorming a theme. After all, you will be looking at it all year along with them!

Here's are a few helpful prompts to come up with a theme for your Glamour Goals:

1. What pop culture references are commonly enjoyed by your team that you could theme your scoreboard with? Think movies, music, famous actors/actresses, sports teams, TV shows, etc.

2. What inside joke does your team, friends, or family have that could be a part of your scoreboard theme?

3. What existing internal communication themes could you leverage to incorporate into your scoreboard?

4. What physical location(s) are highly visible by most or all team members and can be easily updated regularly?

5. If you are a solopreneur, who can you bring into your goal-setting check-ins and celebrations to keep you accountable? These can be accountability partners, a mastermind group, coach, best friend, etc.

Now for the fun part. Get your creative employees or friends together, print out some pics from the Internet or magazines—I highly recommend a Bedazzler and glitter be included in this scoreboard creation extravaganza—and include champagne. You gotta have champagne!

Actually, why stop there? Why not make this a full-fledged girls night in? Make it happen, Bombshell!

When you finish your scoreboard, take a picture of it and share it on my Facebook page or tag me on Instagram, Twitter, or Pinterest. I'd love to see it! Hashtag #GLAMOURGOALS

STEP 6: GUARD YOUR FOCUS

OK, now that you've done both the hard work of setting goals and the fun work of creating a theme for the year's Glamour Goals, it's important that you refuse to be distracted from what you have determined are the most exciting, attractive, and important goals for your business.

First, I want you to commit to avoiding and/or refusing projects and opportunities that take away from focusing on your Glamour Goals. Give a serious once-over of your volunteer obligations. Can you manage all of those *and* still tend to your business and life like a Bombshell should?

Please don't misunderstand me. I am all about volunteering and contributing to organizations you are a part of in leadership roles. However, I often see fempreneurs, especially, become professional volunteers while they simultaneously treat their business more like a hobby. If you have a need to be needed, let me assure you, your business and your customers need you. So, let's get focused, OK?

Ask yourself this question both for current and possible future commitments: *If I say yes to this, what am I saying no to?* If you don't like that answer, then it's time to step away.

Also, I strongly encourage you to become accountable to someone else. This can be an accountability partner, a mastermind, or a small group that meets regularly to check in on each other's progress. Or you can hire a coach or mentor to keep yourself focused.

One of my favorite quotes is the African proverb "If you want to go fast, go alone. If you want to go far, go together." I always say that my success has been three parts support and encouragement from my amazing network and one part piss and vinegar. I highly suggest you try that same recipe! But for all things glittery and glam, please don't skip this step.

When you need a kick in the pants, real talk, or some loving encouragement or support, you will be so glad you created this support system.

STEP 7: MEASURE YOUR RESULTS REGULARLY

Now that you have successfully created and protected your fabulous Glamour Goals, here's what's next to ensure you keep your momentum going strong.

Meet with your team regularly to measure your success, overcome obstacles, and tweak mini goals as needed. Use your Glamour Goals vision and progress board to facilitate this process.

Ask everyone for an update on their mini goals at every meeting. If you don't make it a priority, neither will your team.

If you are a solopreneur, then go through this process with your accountability partner, group, coach, or virtual team and vendors.

Remember: *what gets measured gets done.* If you aren't checking in on your progress, your deadline will sneak up on you and you'll have another year of disappointment. And that's not very glamorous, is it?

On a more positive note, what gets done should be celebrated! So let's talk about creating that atmosphere. Take time with your team or your accountability system to brainstorm ways to recognize your team's and your own mini goal accomplishments. Then come up with even better rewards for accomplishing your ultimate Glamour Goals!

Use your annual Glamour Goal theme to inspire those rewards. For example, if you picked a spa theme, you could give bottles of nail polish, face masks, or pedicure gift certificates to those who achieve their mini goals. However, if someone accomplishes their Glamour Goal, those superstars get to go on the company's spa day outing as the ultimate reward.

Of course, you need to budget these rewards into your financial goals, but what a small investment to keep your team, or even simply you, focused on getting things done.

Because, seriously . . . who is going to miss a spa day?

* * * * * * *

Congratulations! You have completed the Glamour Goals process! I'm so proud of you! Ironing out the details of your most exciting, appealing, and special goals is quite a process. But a true Bombshell who is bold, brave, and unwaveringly confident can see the incredible value in going through with, and then trusting, the process.

For one final recap, here are the seven Glamour Goal steps:

- *Step 1*: Map out every part of your life by month.
- *Step 2*: Identify your Glamour Goals.
- *Step 3*: Test your goals.
- *Step 4*: Create mini goals to support your Glamour Goals.
- *Step 5*: Create (and post) a vision and progress board.
- *Step 6*: Guard your focus.
- *Step 7*: Measure your results regularly.

Be sure to return to this process each year—or at any point—to refresh yourself on the Glamour Goal process. Only you can create bold goals that attract success for your business as you use your God-given gifts to serve others.

Take Action, Bombshell!

*Visit www.thebombshellbusinesswoman.com for free,
downloadable worksheets and resources.*

1. Complete the Glamour Goals process as outlined in this chapter.

2. Do not forget to reward yourself for reaching mini and major Glamour Goals!

Twelve

Your Ideal Customer Profile

Creating an ideal customer profile helps you understand who are you talking to through your marketing, and it helps you carry that message and vibe through to your customer experience.

Before you can decide on your brand fonts, colors, or imagery, let alone your messaging, you need to know who you are trying to attract first. You must ensure your vibe jives with the people most likely to become loyal customers.

The thing is, *If you try to market to everyone, then you successfully market to no one.*

Think about that for a minute.

If I had a dollar for every time someone asked, "What do you think about this logo?" I'd be rich.

My response is always this: "Who is your ideal customer?"

"Anyone who will pay me," they usually respond.

Recruiting all the self-control that is within me, I refrain from an overly dramatic head slap and offer instead: "I'm not sure I'm the right person to ask, since I am not likely someone who would buy that. However, if you can develop a better idea of who would, I can help you focus your branding."

Male small business owners, especially, tend to create brands they are attracted to and reflect their personality, no matter who they are marketing to. It's almost comical to observe the ubermasculine brands out there spitballing their marketing efforts, hoping something sticks. They may be trying to sell to Pinterest-searching suburban moms whose days are filled with animated movies playing in the backseats of their SUVs and shopping for leggings because, at the super-mama-speed pace, leggings are, in fact, proper pants.

These masculine brands don't consider how out of place their branding is in light of the imagery and sensory experiences Suburban Mom has all day, every day. Nothing about their masculine-focused brands appeals or even connects with the supermoms they hope to sell to.

Now that I have you snickering about the boys, I guess it's a good time to say women are pretty guilty on this one too. They select branding elements they think are pretty, offer products and services that would appeal to them and their friends, and refuse to even ask for the sale, because that's "not how they would speak" in everyday life. They are so afraid of leaving someone out of their brand experience that they limit themselves entirely by refusing to "niche," or define exactly, who the heck they are serving.

It's time to stop the insanity. Your ideal customer should be attracted to the brand that rests on the fabulous culture you created, but they don't have to share your personal interests or have the same lifestyle you do.

When I began my first business entity, Planit Nashville, I intended on leveraging my side-hustle event planning company as a college fund for my daughter. I first envisioned helping local busy women plan their small evening and weekend events in my spare time. However, through a series of good decisions and strategic alliances, I ended up running a full-time, nonstop, very successful celebrity event planning company. We worked with internationally renowned country music artists, as well as other entertainment industry clients, such as record labels and movie studios.

I assure you, when I had my celebrity event planning company, nothing about my life looked like my end customer's life. However, the values that represented my brand aligned with the fast-paced, glamorous yet down-to-earth world of the country music industry.

We were so busy in 2008 and 2009 that my strategic partner and I worked practically round the clock, from early in the morning to late at night. Yes, that is also a time period widely noted as the worst economic downturn since the Great Depression. So how were we able to have explosive growth in a terrible economy? We appealed to our ideal customer and became known as a trusted, well-oiled machine that respected the privacy and responded to the unique challenges of our A-list clientele.

Think about all the different people who represent your customer base (or hopeful customer base) who are attracted to your Business Mojo. Identifying their common characteristics allows you, in turn, to attract more customers just like them. Imagine how awesome it would be if you could recreate the customer who is your best raving fan, who is super fun to do business with, and who spends the most money with you. Now imagine if that one person, who shares the same characteristics as their peer group, brought all of their friends, and then their friends brought their friends, and so on, to do business with you.

An ideal customer profile directs your overall messaging, which helps you craft your content (like social media or blog posts), focuses your offerings, and helps you identify . . . drum roll, please . . . how to solve the problems of your customers in a way that speaks to their specific needs and concerns. (Don't you love it when we come full circle?)

What's more, being able to tell the story of your ideal customer will enable you to empower marketing and branding vendors to maintain the integrity of your brand, keeping your brand experience consistent. Also, when leveraging traditional advertising like magazine or radio ads or new media like Facebook ads or Pay Per Click (PPC), you will know exactly what parameters you need to use to guide the placement of your ads for maximum exposure to the people who are most likely to buy from you.

It's perfectly acceptable to have multiple profiles for your business, as your business likely has various markets that you pull from. In fact, it is wise to segment your audience in your marketing, such as with email marketing or direct mail marketing. For example, a real estate agent would not want to send the same open house postcard to a potential home buyer looking for a starter home as they would a potential multimillion-dollar home buyer. It's a waste of time and money and, ultimately, shows the potential home buyers the agent doesn't care about their specific needs.

Likewise, how you market to potential customers might look very different from how to market to existing customers. For example, a fitness center might run dual promotions: new members get their first month free while existing members get a month of free dues with a referral. Imagine how an existing long-term member would feel if they saw a stranger to the business was getting a benefit they did not get after years of consistently paying their membership dues?

Perhaps even more fun (especially if you involve your team) is creating a negative customer profile. This profile describes exactly who you don't want as a customer so you can weed them out of your marketing and ensure your sales associates do not focus their time pursuing them. You could not want a particular type of customer for a variety of reasons, including the fact they may take a lot of time and energy from a customer service standpoint without a return on those investments in the form of revenue. Or it could be that they are not ready for, or are too advanced for, your product or service. Sometimes a customer might be too price sensitive for your offering, or maybe they expect too much from your brand versus what you are willing or able to offer. Understanding who *isn't* your ideal customer sometimes helps you better clarify who is.

HOW TO IDENTIFY YOUR IDEAL CUSTOMER

If you're a new business or a soon-to-be business, it's helpful to interview the people you think would be your ideal customer. Also, it is helpful to look at your peer and aspirant brands to borrow their customer attributes. You have to start somewhere, so use whatever data you can come up with. Just don't make it up as you go!

If you are an established business, you can:

- Interview your best customers
- Survey your database or email list
- Distribute in-store surveys
- Consult your social media analytics
- Analyze your website analytics
- Ask your sales team or employees who know your customers best

To make things even more real, find a photo online of someone you think represents each of your Ideal Customer

Profiles and give each of them a name. You will find that while you're in meetings with your team or marketing vendors, you'll hear things like, "I don't think Judy would buy that," or, "Paul is not going to respond to that ad." You will start to immerse yourself in the lives of these ideal customers, which will only strengthen your brand, your marketing, and your customer experience.

The Council of American Survey Research Organizations estimated spending on marketing research in the United States reached $6.7 billion in 2010, with worldwide spending nearing $18.9 billion.[1] Don't you think you can invest a little sweat equity to figure out who the best customers are for your business?

Take Action, Bombshell!

Visit www.thebombshellbusinesswoman.com for free, downloadable worksheets and resources.

Answer the following questions to craft your Ideal Customer Profile. To keep things easy, I refer to your ideal customer as "her," although I realize your ideal customer could be a man as well.

Basic Information
- What is your ideal customer's name?
- How old is she?
- What does she look like? (Describe her physical features and personal style.)
- Is she married, single, or divorced?
- How many children does she have?
- What city and state does she call home?

Professional
- What is her occupation?
- What is her personal annual income?
- What is her annual household income?
- What professional conferences and events does she attend?
- What professional organizations does she actively participate in?
- What experts does she follow?

Personal
- List her five main priorities in life in order of their importance.

Spiritual
- What does she currently believe about her life?
- What about her past holds her back from getting what she wants?
- Who is her hero?

Online Interests
- What are her favorite blogs?
- What are her favorite social media sites?
- What Pinterest boards does she follow?
- What Facebook pages does she like?
- What does she Google?
- What YouTube video did she last share?

Entertainment
- What are her favorite television shows?
- What are her favorite books?
- What are her favorite movies?
- What magazines does she read?

- What is her favorite way to spend her free time?
- What is her guilty pleasure?

Lifestyle
- What type of home does she have (homeowner, rents house, rents apartment, multiple homes, etc.)?
- What car does she drive, or what type of transportation does she use if she doesn't drive (Uber, subway, taxi, bus, etc.)?
- If she could eat as much of one thing as she wanted and never gain any weight, what would that be?
- What's her favorite way to exercise—or does she?
- Where is her dream vacation?
- What brands are her favorite to shop for?

Journal Entry

Write a journal entry from your ideal customer's perspective that she writes the night before she possibly does business with you for the first time.

Thirteen

Getting Attention with a Red Lipstick Marketing Plan

You can put a lot of time and energy into your makeup and not change the way you look all that much. Or you put that same amount of effort in and you end up not looking like yourself at all, shocking people when you are fresh-faced. (Watch a contour YouTube video and you'll know exactly what I mean.) The thing about making makeup really count is you have to have the know-how to properly apply it, and you have to have the resources to buy all the makeup to begin with.

So what happens when you apply just a little bit of makeup and then some red lipstick?

You get a lot of "pop," or impact, for a limited amount of effort.

What I've found over the years of working with female business owners is that they spend the majority of their time in the day, for that day, dealing with daily operations; their focus is on the business at hand and not putting together some complex marketing plan. They usually don't they have the resources to hire it out, either.

If that sounds like you, that's OK. Maybe one day you will reach the point where you can hire someone to plan and execute your marketing strategy. Or maybe you won't because you don't want your business to get that big!

When I was younger, my friends teased me that I would not even go to the mailbox without big sunglasses and red lipstick, so I would at least appear pulled together. I know I barely got my bra on, but what anyone driving by saw was a woman who was polished, had her act together, and was consistent.

And that's what I want for your Red Lipstick Marketing Blueprint.

Yes, this is where marketing professionals would dive into the "Four Ps of Marketing," explain the difference between strategies and tactics, and present you with a thirty-two-page marketing plan. And they should, because they focus on marketing full-time, every day. I'm certain, in the same way, a makeup artist can put on her full face in a lot less time than you can.

But for most businesses trying to keep the everyday going, and who are not in a position to hire a marketing professional or firm, there is simply no need to spend hours layering expensive, excessive makeup on your business. Just apply a little "red lipstick" and get a ton of attention without unnecessary effort.

Remember, all of your marketing efforts should support your Business Mojo Statement—and again, it meets at the intersection of what lights you up, what makes you unique from your competition, and what brings in those dolla dolla billz, y'all.

If you are marketing products or services that aren't really bringing in that much money, then you need to take a closer look at your return on your investment and whether you are pouring money into your efforts or time, because time is money.

Think about Domino's Pizza. Yes, they offer hot wings, breadsticks, and soft drinks, but what do you see commercials about? What do you see in their print advertising? What do you see in online ads or even on billboards?

Pizza!

They are not trying to get you in the door by selling breadsticks. They start with the pizza because that is their mojo. That is their money maker.

So just as Domino's does with its pizza and side items, lure your customer in with your profit center, and then upsell them on your other complementary offerings.

Then, of course, you need to ensure your marketing plan supports your Glamour Goals. Creating a plan to bring in more business in a way that does not ultimately support your annual goals is fighting against yourself.

So with your "pizza" and your "glamour" top of mind, let's consider your next three months' marketing plan. Yes, we are only going to tackle your exact marketing plan three months at a time because business changes quickly. *Life* changes quickly. So while you do want to have an operating plan for your entire fiscal year, creating a marketing plan three months at a time allows you to pivot when you can clearly see what is working and what isn't, and what is going on in your local—or even the national and global—economy, depending on what type of business you have. You can see what people are responding to, what's trending, and you can be more nimble, which is one of the greatest assets of small business.

RED LIPSTICK MARKETING STEP 1: DETERMINE WHAT YOU PLAN TO PROMOTE

Using your Glamour Goals and keeping your Business Mojo in mind, focus on no more than three products or services you plan to promote in the next three months. Keep it simple. Don't try to boil the ocean, and do keep your branding consistent. Furthermore, keep in mind that when Domino's runs a special on its hot wings, you never lose sight of the fact that it's a pizza joint.

RED LIPSTICK MARKETING STEP 2: PLAN TO MEASURE YOUR SUCCESS

Determine how you are going to measure your success. Choose two to three time-bound, measurable objectives you want to achieve through your marketing efforts. You want to be able to say, for example, "I will know I am successful if these three things happen."

For instance, the following companies could define success in these ways.

Fitness Center
- Attract an average of twenty nonmembers each month to take a free class.

- Acquire five new members each month via current member referrals.

- Upgrade two memberships each month from an individual membership to a couple or family membership.

Boutique
- Increase email list by seventy-five new qualified emails each month.

- Consistently increase average sales by 10 percent.

- Increase total monthly store revenue to $23,000 by the end of the quarter.

Public Speaker
- Set up three consultations with potential new clients each week.

- Submit eighteen speaking proposals by the end of the quarter.

- Acquire five new paid speaking engagements by the end of the quarter.

Side note: Do not measure your marketing impact based on "exposure." You cannot feed your family on "exposure." If you cannot tie your marketing efforts to actual dollars that the electric company will accept, it's time to adjust your plan.

You may decide to put daily, weekly, and/or monthly measurements in place, but the key to this step is *doing it*! If your plan is not working, pivot. If it is working, do more of it! A simple checklist or spreadsheet works just fine. Keep it simple, Sista!

THE THREE TYPES OF MARKETING ACTIVITIES: ACTIVE, PASSIVE, AND KEEP IN TOUCH

There are three basic types of activities you should focus on in your Red Lipstick Marketing Plan when trying to generate sales for your business: Active, Passive, and Keep In Touch. Let's break them down by each type, then select which activities from each type you plan to use in the next quarter.

If you can do more than the recommended activities, great! But since you're learning and just getting started, it's better to do a few things well than many things poorly! It's also important to choose activities that are mostly easy to manage with your current knowledge, and then only one or two things that are a challenge.

If you are not techy at all, I don't suggest you load up your Red Lipstick Marketing Plan with social media plans, YouTube videos, and SEO (search engine optimization) strategies. It's not going to work. Maybe you're a raging extrovert. Your best plan might be to decide to start speaking locally as an expert, bump up your networking game, hold an open house or in-store event, partner with other complementary (but not competing) businesses, and then carve out time to map out the changes you should make on your website.

Remember what you revealed about yourself while developing your personal brand. Operate primarily in your strengths, then integrate things a little bit at a time that take you out of your comfort zone (or what might be considered your zone of genius).

Active Marketing Activities

Active strategies ensure you are going out into the world and asking people to become your customer, or that you are actively asking your current customers to take the next step with you. Pick three to five activities from this category to get out there and seek business.

Active Marketing Activities
(Choose three to five)

X	Active Marketing Activities	Budget	Time Frame
	Speaking Engagements		
	Open Houses or Live Events		
	Webinars/Google Hangouts/ Teleclasses/Teleseminars/		

	Introduction Letters		
	Networking Opportunities and Groups		
	Workshops		
	Joint Venture Partners/ Strategic Alliances (online and in person)		
	Business to Business Visits		
	Cold Calls		
	Advertising (traditional or online)		
	Social Media (No, you cannot hide behind this alone!)		
	Writing (for a magazine, guest blogging, trade publi-cation, etc.)		
	Direct Mail		
	PR Ops (news stories, being interviewed by media outlets, podcasts, etc.)		
	Videos		
	Live Streaming		
	Hosting a Podcast		
	Blogging		
	Billboard Ad		
	Direct Mail		
	Sponsoring an Event		
	Sending Out Promotional Items		
	Text Promotions		
	Email Marketing Campaigns		
	Other:		

Passive Marketing Activities

Passive activities complement your active activities when potential customers seek you out by preparing you to convert prospects into customers.

When you invite someone over to dinner, you clean your house, prepare a menu, and perhaps even have glassware out to graciously offer them a cocktail (or mocktail) as soon as they arrive. You're prepared.

The same should go for your business. You need to have your passive marketing game in place to ensure your marketing home is prepared to receive guests.

Of course, as discussed, it starts with consistent branding. If someone seeks you out, you should make them feel the same way about your business through each and every interaction.

Is your website ready for a visitor? What do you want them to do when they get there? Book an appointment? Download a free resource or coupon? Follow you on Instagram?

What about online business listings? If someone Googles you, do you have a Google Place set up? What about Yelp? Manta? Travel sites? City- or regional-specific sites?

Or maybe optimizing your SEO is where you need to focus so people can easily find you to begin with. What is your ideal customer Googling when looking for a business like yours?

The bottom line in this section of preparing your house for visitors is ensuring that when someone is trying to find out more about you, not only can they, but they get the same message you are sending people you are actively seeking business from. The following areas are opportunities for you to entice prospects with your brand experience. Select two to three ways from this category to tidy up your house and set the table for guests.

Passive Marketing Activities
(Choose two to three)

X	Passive Marketing Activities	Budget	Time Frame
	Website (to include list-building give-away, sales pages, etc.)		
	Business Cards		
	Online Business Listings		
	Brochure		
	Letterhead		
	Signage		
	Search Engine Optimization		
	Other:		

Keep In Touch Marketing Activities

The time to market yourself is *all of the time.* Every person in the market for your product or service might be ready to buy from you . . . at nearly any point. You want to be top-of-mind when somebody needs your kind of service or product, so you must consistently work for that opportunity. The way to do that is to stay in touch with your previous, existing, and potential customers.

Just think of all the women who missed one or two cut or color appointments with their stylist in the past year because their schedule got out of hand before their roots did. Sure, they called, desperately looking for a spot on their stylist's book, but it was still a week or two past their own comfort level before they could get in. That is hundreds, or even thousands, of dollars of missed revenue a stylist could have earned had she or he had a system in place to stay top-of-mind with clients.

These days, attention spans are limited and lives are packed. You have to be sure you are staying a priority alongside your customer's work and family responsibilities and whatever is going on behind the scenes with *The Real Housewives*.

To make sure you don't fall to the bottom of the priority list, select one to three ways to proactively keep in touch with your current, potential, and even past customers.

Keep In Touch Marketing Activities
(Choose one to three)

X	Keep In Touch Marketing Activities	Budget	Time Frame
	E-newsletter		
	Blog Delivered to Your Email List		
	Printed Newsletter		
	Follow-Up Calls to Potential, New, and Dormant Clients		
	Direct Mail		
	Email Nurture Sequence		
	Text Campaigns		
	Other:		

To recap, there are three types of marketing activities in the Red Lipstick Marketing Plan: Active (you actively seek out business), Passive (you are ready to convert when business comes to you), and Keep In Touch (you stay top-of-mind so you're the first person a prospect comes to when they need your kind of help).

You want to create goals in each of those areas and decide what success would look like—what outcome you're driving for through each of your activities. Then you want to measure your success regularly, as well as measure the overall impact at the end of the three-month period, and then reassess what to do for the next quarter.

Again, you may need to give some things a little more time to gain traction, or you may not want to change anything because it's working so well. Most likely, you'll want to tweak a thing or two to elevate your results or accommodate a busy season, slow season, or holiday that impacts your industry or area specifically.

Most importantly, remember to leave the primer, concealer, contouring, false eyelashes, and your thirty-two shades of neutral eyeshadow in your proverbial vanity. To set yourself up for success, you need to be real about what you can commit to *consistently*. As you improve your marketing skills and habits, you can then learn how to create more complex plans or even be in a position to hire a team member or marketing firm to handle all of the "strategery."

Until you're ready for all that, just keep it simple and pull out that trusty red lipstick for a big impact with limited effort!

Take Action, Bombshell!

Visit www.thebombshellbusinesswoman.com for free, downloadable worksheets and resources.

- *What are one to three products or services you are trying to sell or promote through the next three months?*
1.
2.

3.

- *List two to three specific, measurable, time-bound goals for your Red Lipstick Marketing Plan.*

  1.

  2.

  3.

- *Write down three to five tactics from the Active Marketing Activities menu.*

  1.

  2.

  3.

  4.

  5.

- *Write down two to three tactics from the Passive Marketing Activities menu.*

  1.

  2.

  3.

- *Write down one to three tactics from the Keep In Touch Marketing Activities menu.*

  1.

  2.

  3.

Fourteen

How to Network Like a Lady Boss

We've all heard the famous Jim Rohn quote: "You are the average of the five people you spend the most time with."[1] But have you ever really contemplated who those five people are and if they are the five people who should be most influential in your life? Yeah, it feels a little harsh to start analyzing friends, family, and colleagues—in fact, it might feel a little self-serving at first.

If you want to be a true Bombshell, a bold, brave, and unwaveringly confident fempreneur, then you need to build a support system that helps you be your best. So let's take a moment to first inventory your inner circle and categorize them into the Good, the Bad, and the Ugly.

THE GOOD

The type of people you should be spending the majority of your time with to become your best self (personally, professionally, financially, and beyond) should be of excellent influence. Invest your time, energy, intellect, and emotion into them, and your return will be exponential.

They should lift you up and encourage you, even when you fail, and teach you many things, be they life lessons or business skills. I've always said we can't all experience everything, but we can all learn from each other's experiences, making learning curves shorter and pitfalls avoidable.

Good influences are positive, and they see the good in even bad situations. They are problem solvers who don't fall victim to circumstances. They are likely to introduce you to even more successful people because success attracts success.

These are the people who are worth spending your limited time with. What you pour into them will produce fruit.

THE BAD

The Bad aren't people you need to ditch entirely, but you need to limit your time with them. We all have that person we want to maintain a positive relationship with. But you know that they suck the life out of you with every passing minute you spend together. They whine about things instead of making them better. They are complainers who see the bad in everything—even good situations. Nothing is ever good enough for them! They are unmotivated and happy with status quo, and they have limited plans and virtually no goals. You want to severely limit your time with these people. Use your influence when you can, but don't let them pull you down to their level. Start to spend less and less time with them until it's just natural that it stays that way.

THE UGLY

The Ugly are the people you need to cut out of your life immediately without notice. They are mentally, physically, or emotionally abusive, or just plain trouble. They try to use words, social engineering, manipulation, or force to control you. They are people who make you feel bad for moving ahead toward your greatness because you will then leave them behind. They are the gossips. (And if they talk about others around you, you better believe they are talking about you to others.) Your day will come when they overshare about your business or speak negatively of you with others as well—if they haven't already. What's more, you should avoid anyone who regularly and systematically makes you feel less than who you are or keeps you from becoming who you want to become. Let's be real: these people are cancerous.

Back to the concept of learning lessons other people already learned the hard way: believe me when I say I am offering this perspective from experience. It was especially hard for me to decide who I needed to include on Team Amber as a young mother. My world, priorities, and goals shifted exponentially from those of my peers, at sixteen, and I made several mistakes with the Bad and the Ugly.

Fortunately, I reprioritized the good people in my life and put them where they belonged: in the top five. And my good five went to ten, and then fifteen, and so on. I am here to tell you that there is no way I could have found my success today without the support of the good people in my life, both personally and professionally. Because I started investing in wiser relationships, I am now an absurdly wealthy woman—if blessings, fulfillment, and joy are measured as wealth.

The bottom line is, "No man [or woman] is an island."[2] You can't do life on your own. So I challenge you, today, to inventory your influences and decide who you need to make investments in and which shady people you need to move away from to keep your business and life charging toward success.

WHERE TO FIND THE "GOOD PEOPLE" FOR YOUR NETWORK

While you know you have to limit your time with the Bad and run from the Ugly, what if you don't have enough good people in your life to build a solid support system? Here are ways you can accomplish that.

Volunteering

I always tell people I'm mentoring that they need to go volunteer. It's good for the world to help a cause that is bigger than yourself. But it also opens you up to getting to know other people who are like-minded in helping others (including you, potentially). Further, most nonprofits have boards that feature successful, influential people. If you are a standout volunteer, those super successful board members will notice you and potentially open doors for you that would otherwise be beyond your own influence.

Networking Events

Another opportunity would be industry or otherwise related networking events. Just go and take the pressure off of yourself. You don't have to know what to say about yourself to make you sound incredibly interesting. Simply focus on who is there, what they do, and how you can help them. Most people like to talk about themselves, so get them going and you'll make new friends quickly!

Other Professional Events

Attend conferences or seminars, book signings, or go to any event where people you want to be like hang out. Usually people who attend such events are driven, interested in learning, and, importantly, looking to meet new people too.

Clubs and Organizations

Whether you are focused on clubs geared toward female professionals, tech heads, bloggers, social media professionals, golfers, gardeners, or swimmers, it is likely that there is a club or Meetup in your area that has people with interests similar to yours.

Social Media

If all of that doesn't seem manageable, social media is easy, nonthreatening, and can lead to real-life social opportunities. Trust me. I have made many friends with whom I share great relationships to this day, have traveled with, and celebrated special occasions with . . . who, yes, I first met on social media. Facebook has oodles of free groups to join, as does LinkedIn. On Twitter you can get involved in Twitter chats focused on your industry or interests. The opportunities are endless.

These ideas are truly scratching the surface. No matter the method, the important thing is to just start meeting people. So start now by brainstorming where people you want to be like hang out. When you have a good list, try them until you realize that the five people you spend the most time with really rock your face off!

HOW TO WORK A NETWORKING EVENT LIKE A LADY BOSS

But what if I'm not any good at networking, Amber?

Well, I admit it. I'm a people addict, and I don't want to quit!

However, whether networking comes naturally for you or is some seriously scary stuff, it is important to be intentional about every networking opportunity you decide to pursue. To make it a little easier, here are some basic dos and don'ts of networking.

Networking Dos

- Decide what your purpose is prior to the event. Want to meet new people—any people? How about find new opportunities for your business? Or maybe find people to collaborate with? Be clear with yourself so you spend your time wisely.

- Ask your new friend about their business and life first. It will help warm you up to this whole talk-to-a-stranger thing. (And seriously, if there truly are just six degrees of separation from Kevin Bacon, there are like two degrees from anyone in your hometown.) In other words, if you are networking in a small- to medium-sized city, you likely know many mutual friends and that can instaconnect you to the bestie fast track!

- Come up with three talking points prior to the networking opportunity, so if you only get a short amount of time with someone key, you can spit out what you want people to remember about you. Like, if you had five minutes on *Oprah*, what would you have to say to feel like you maxed out the opportunity?

- Follow up with people quickly following the event so you don't find a stack of cards in your desk drawer three months later—all a blatant reminder of wasted opportunity! Ouch!

Networking Don'ts

- *Please* don't say, "Yeah, girl. Let's network." Because that's what you are currently doing! #awkward

- Don't start a conversation by shoving a business card in someone's face. It's just bad manners.

- Don't (for the love of SEC Football and everything else

that is holy) put *anyone* on your email list following the event without their permission. That is legit illegal. Consult the FTC's CAN-SPAM Act[3] if you don't believe me.

- Don't skip out because of a lame reason, such as not having a friend to go with you (you're an adult, you can do this), crummy weather (if I can rock an umbrella the day of a blowout, you can brave the rain too), or simply because you're having a long day already. Because when you are sitting there a month from now without any traction in your networking goals, you will have wished you found your big girl panties and sucked it up. (You're welcome for that velvet machete real talk.)

A NOTE TO INTROVERTS ABOUT NETWORKING

If you are an introvert, I know your idea of an amazing evening is being all by yourself in your home after an exhausting day of interacting with people. That's you and there is nothing wrong with how you recharge your batteries. Here are a few tips, just for you, to help keep you in the networking game as painlessly as possible.

- Schedule quiet, alone time regularly for the week leading up to the networking event. This will help you store up some dealing-with-people juice. Likewise, if at all possible, schedule some down time the day after the event so you can restore the energy you generously shared with your new friends.

- Research as much as you can before the event so you can take your time figuring it all out. If the guest list is posted online, check out the social profiles of the guests and see what they are about and learn more about the hosts or the sponsoring organization. The more you can absorb prior to the event, the less you will have to process information quickly while also dealing with the people in front of you. Can you say, "Win!"

- Use your superpower: introverts are typically great listeners! Not to mention, you probably are great at reading body language and understanding what isn't being said. You will be able to quickly assess who is worth following up with and who is more of a self-promoter or leech. Lucky you. The bonus is, the next time you see someone, you will remember something super thoughtful about them; an extrovert focused on chatting more than listening might not catch the same level of depth. So basically you have the potential to really wow your new friends and make them feel super special. Again, lucky you!

Follow these tips, my introverted friend, and you will be able to build a powerful network without bankrupting your energy reserves. And make no mistake: if you want to make it as an entrepreneur, you simply can't do it on your own. This is a nonnegotiable!

Take Action, Bombshell!

Visit www.thebombshellbusinesswoman.com for free, downloadable worksheets and resources.

Create your networking action plan by answering the following questions to expand your reach and fill your life with people you can invest in and who can help you reach your goals.

1. *Decide who you need in your network.*

- Potential customers
- Referral sources
- Influencers (who can connect me to other people who can help me succeed)
- Strategic partners (complementary, not competing, businesses I can comingle audiences with, ones willing to share advertising costs, cohost events, cross-promote on social media and via email marketing, and more)

2. *Select where you will likely find those people.*

- Volunteer opportunities (serving on boards, committing to volunteer days, serving on nonprofit committees, etc.)
- Networking events (local industry-specific events, Chamber of Commerce public events, Meetup.com, Eventbrite, Facebook events, etc.)
- Other professional events (conferences, seminars, book signings, charity events)
- Clubs and organizations (entrepreneur or industry-specific clubs, civic groups, hobby groups, country clubs, health clubs, etc.)
- Social media (Facebook groups, LinkedIn groups, Twitter chats, etc.)

3. *Decide which networking events you will attend.*

Now that you know who you need in your network and what networking opportunities you can take advantage of, list five specific in-person or online events you will attend in the next sixty days.

Networking Events

Event Name	Event Location	Event Date	Start Time

4. *Create an event plan. For each of these events, answer the following questions to prepare yourself.*

- What is your purpose for attending this event?

- What can you offer people you meet that is not self-serving and can realistically be done with your available time (e.g., help them connect with others, share business processes, point them to industry resources you've found helpful, etc.)?

- What are your three key talking points that allow you to be prepared when the conversation turns to you?

- How are you going to follow up with the individuals you want to engage with? (Remember, even if you meet someone online, you can schedule a Skype, Zoom, or Google Hangout to next-level your professional relationship.)

Fifteen

How to Work with Creative Vendors

When it comes time to work with vendors to help you execute your Red Lipstick Marketing Plan, it's important to have a plan on the front end to ensure you have a smooth experience and ultimately an impressive end result.

I have managed and worked with creative professionals such as photographers, website designers, graphic designers, videographers, direct mail professionals, writers, and more for many, many years. Thank goodness my Botox® hides just how many years that has been!

"Creative" professionals come in many different packages and speak the language of art. It can be frustrating for an analytical person, for example, to communicate with an expressive person who "sees" more than they can tally. Creatives are not, in general (certainly not as a rule), linear thinkers; rather, they tend to think in imagery and concepts.

You may not have a huge budget to accomplish lofty

branding and marketing goals, but don't let that stop you from moving forward as best you can today. Theodore Roosevelt said, "Do what you can, with what you have, where you are."[1]

Business is fluid and you can always improve and progress as your time and financial resources allow, and as your learning curve shortens. Keep that in mind as I give the following advice.

HOW TO FIND THE PERFECT CREATIVE VENDOR

You want to find someone with the best experience you can afford, preferably with experience in your industry and even, specifically, with experience in your niche. Ask friends and colleagues who they have enjoyed working with and why. Look for examples of their work before narrowing down who you plan to interview for your project. If you cannot find anything that looks like your brand in their examples, you won't likely find it in the work they do for you either. For example, if their portfolio is full of edgy brands with controversial messages or bold designs, it's not likely they would do their best work for a soft, innocent-type brand that uses flowery language and ultrafeminine visuals. Don't try to force-fit collaboration; rather, look for natural fits. Once you find a handful of vendors (whether individuals or a firm), pick three options and schedule initial meetings so you can determine if it could be a good opportunity for both sides.

In the interview process, get clear on what you will receive in value for the investment you will make. Again, cheaper does not always equal better. Ask about how they work and the process you will go through from start to finish. Be clear about your vision and goals, as well as your work style and timeline.

Ask for references. Testimonials on a website can be totally legit, but they can also reflect a friend's rave reviews. Besides, testimonials give a high-level review of the work, but a conversation can reveal how the work got done.

> ### Bombshell Quick Tip
> Taking a risk on up-and-comers who want to build their portfolios could save you a ton of money while supporting the budding businesses of others; however, you also may end up with subpar results and have to start over with a more experienced person. Tread carefully here.

HOW TO EFFECTIVELY WORK WITH A CREATIVE VENDOR

Once you have selected your vendor, do not move forward without agreeing on the terms of your engagement—and putting them in writing. Do not blindly sign their contract. Understand what you are getting in the deal, including who actually owns the intellectual property they will produce for you. Unless your vendor specifically transfers copyright ownership to you, ownership of creative work, by default, is retained by the actual creator. If you want the right to reproduce or even sell what you paid for, you want to be sure there is "work made for hire" or "work for hire" language in the contract.

Again, since intellectual property is being shared, you may want to include a mutual nondisclosure in your agreement, so you both promise not to share confidential and proprietary information or trade secrets (like how the other does business) with third parties.

Also, be sure dispute resolution is covered in your agreement. For example, this will outline things like whether you will start with mediation, and who will bear the cost of reasonable legal fees.

Even if you are doing business with friends, have an agreement in place. It only serves to strengthen your relationship and establish trust. You certainly want to avoid that awkward moment when you don't know exactly what you are paying for or what you are supposed to get. But . . . you're dealing with a friend, so you just accept what you're given. All the while, your friend is thinking they did their best work and delivered on the promise.

I'm not an attorney, nor do I play one on TV, so do your research and consult the US Copyright Office, layperson-friendly legal sites like LegalZoom.com or, ideally, build a long-term relationship with a local business attorney. I'm merely outlining some of the common pitfalls I see Bombshells fall into.

Once you begin working with a creative vendor, be as clear as you can on the front end so you empower them to deliver on your expectations, and so your timeline does not slow down with avoidable revisions.

Here is where it all comes together, Bombshell! Begin these relationships with sharing your company culture and brand messaging, as well as your visual brand standards, if those already exist. Share your Ideal Customer Profile. Your creative vendors should be as clear as you are about who you are, what you offer, what makes you different, and who you are talking to in your marketing. Help them tell your story by providing them with knowledge.

You can also create separate inspiration boards on Pinterest, for example, of websites you think would inspire your own look, photography styles and poses you want considered for your upcoming photo shoot, videos you would like to emulate in your own video shoot, logos that feel right to you, or just brands in general you believe can communicate your style. This is especially helpful for anyone who has a hard time communicating visual or emotional concepts, and it is also a perfect way to communicate visually, and well, with a visual communicator.

If you're not the Pinterest type, you can always make a vision board in a simple Word document or in a free online design program like Canva or PicMonkey. And since I promised I would shoot you straight, I'll even admit to drawing stick figures and submitting them to "show" what I was trying to achieve. Don't be too proud. Remember: "Do what you can, with what you have, where you are."

Finally, remember that any creative development is an ongoing conversation. Give prompt and direct feedback, explaining the "why" for both your positive and negative opinions. This will help your vendors quickly get to know your preferences. Show respect for your vendors and honor the gifts they're sharing with you. In the same way, be clear and dignified when your expectations are not met. Like you, they're in business to use their natural abilities to serve other people. They want to make you happy.

If you choose the right vendors, your collective and sincere motives should establish both trust and grace on both sides of the relationship. Remember that businesses are made up of humans like you. They aren't going to be perfect and they will need encouragement, clarification, and correction to deliver their best. Likewise, be open to the feedback you receive from them regarding your actions and how they impact the project. Indecisiveness, changing your vision, holding up deadlines, and not communicating effectively—these are all ways you can create complications for yourself. Work with your vendors with the perspective that you are all moving toward the same goal. Supporting their efforts supports your efforts. It's that simple.

As your business grows, you will find yourself working with more and more creative vendors to strengthen your brand and expand your marketing reach. Even if you delegate that responsibility, ultimately you are the one responsible for how your brand is portrayed. Using these lessons, your Bombshell business will always be consistent, relevant, and "on brand."

Take Action, Bombshell!

Visit www.thebombshellbusinesswoman.com for free, downloadable worksheets and resources.

1. *What is your monthly marketing budget?*

2. *What type of marketing vendors do you need to collaborate with for your business?*

3. *What is your most urgent marketing project (e.g., website update, newspaper ad, logo)?*

4. *Who are your top three marketing vendor options for your most urgent project?*

5. *Research copyright laws at either of these websites that may apply to you before agreeing to contractual terms:*
   - https://www.copyright.gov/title17/
   - legalzoom.com

Sixteen

Captivating Customer Service

Did you know that acquiring a new customer is five to twenty-five times more expensive than retaining an existing one? If you believe the *Harvard Business Review*, among countless studies in numerous industries, that is a fact you can take to the bank.[1]

So if you want to go out there and blow all your money unnecessarily to acquire new customers, go on with your bad self. I'm just laying out the facts here so you'll perk up and listen to me as I'm going through how important customer service is to retain the customers you already have.

Yet customer retention isn't the only reason to invest in amazing customer service. Making sure your word-of-mouth marketing is on point is a pretty big reason too.

After all, happy customers tell their friends. Unhappy customers tell the world.

Just scroll through your Facebook page. How many times do you see someone going on and on about their positive experience with a company? A few people might politely agree in the comments. It's a blip in your newsfeed and doesn't draw that much attention.

Compare that to when someone complains about a business. Not only is it the length of a novel, the follow-up comments are astonishing. Suddenly, disgruntled customers have a platform, and by golly, they're going to use it! Everyone jumps on the bandwagon. That post, with a high level of engagement, trips the Facebook algorithm, and it's the post that hangs out at the top of your newsfeed for two days, no matter how many times you refresh.

Exceptional customer service proactively manages your brand and reactively can turn upset customers into raving fans based on how you handled their complaint.

As important as your Red Lipstick Marketing Plan is, its ongoing success is ultimately dependent on your ability to keep your customers happy.

Aristotle said, "We are what we repeatedly do. Excellence, then, is not an act but a habit."[2]

Customer service has everything to do with consistency, systems, training, and the *habits* you and your team create. It begins with your company culture and follows through to the tools and resources you use each day that are unique to your business.

You—and your employees if you have them—should all be singing the same song, in the same key, the same way no matter who their audience is. If one person has an extraordinary experience, the next person should have an extraordinary experience. It's when you don't repeatedly do the same thing for everyone that you go off the rails.

You see, every single person who comes into your establishment walks in with a wagon of experiences and a bucket of expectations.

Let's say you own a day spa. Imagine somebody walking

into your business for her 11 a.m. appointment, pulling a little Radio Flyer® wagon full of experiences from her entire life. It carries every single massage, body wrap, and facial memory she's ever had. What's more, it's also full of how she's been treated throughout her life: how her mother spoke to her, how she was picked last in PE, everything her ex-husband did and did not do, and more. It's filled with every time she genuinely felt beautiful, memories of her sophomore English teacher who made her feel valued, and the power she felt when she finally found the confidence to tell her boss she deserved a raise.

In the other hand, she carries her bucket of expectations. This is her empty bucket that she expects you to fill to the top to meet her expectations. Those expectations come from all the experiences she's pulling in that wagon.

Now that you understand the story of the person in front of you has expectations based on a lifetime of experiences, how patient can you now be? When she is upset beyond reason because her massage had to be cancelled at the last minute, what do you think has gone on in that wagon of hers that made her react so extremely? What part of her bucket of expectations do you really need to fill? *That* is the question.

So how do we begin dealing with this woman's wagon—and her bucket?

SMILE—ALWAYS

Always, always, *always* smile. If you're on the phone, you should be smiling and that person should feel the energy even if it's over the phone. If you're writing an email or responding to a website inquiry, you better be smiling. If you're smiling, then your mind-set is starting out positive. Even if you're ticked off at them because of something that they said that irked you—which customers have the darndest habit of doing sometimes—you're still smiling. Doing so naturally helps you respond in a positive and professional manner.

BUILD APPROPRIATE RAPPORT

I say build "appropriate" rapport because sometimes, especially in service-based industries, it's easy to get familiar and friendly with your customers. Friend or not, be careful not to cross the line, forgetting they are paying you to provide them with a product or service, not to hang out.

Conversely, be sure you treat each of your customers like people. To be even more clear, if you have a customer appointment at eleven o'clock, *never* refer to that human being as your "eleven o'clock." If Janet is coming at eleven, then *Janet* is coming at eleven o'clock. Get in the habit of talking about humans, not time slots, because the people who are coming into your businesses are humans with wagons and buckets. They are not a box to check off in the middle of your day's to-dos. Janet may be coming to your establishment at that exact hour to pick up her wedding cake. So, while on your schedule it's your "eleven o'clock," to your customer this is a moment to treasure as it relates, perhaps, to the most important day of her life.

USE EMPATHY

Walk a mile in your customers' stilettos or loafers. Try to understand where they are in the moment. They could be stressed out or limited on time or, conversely, looking for a celebratory experience. Put yourself in their shoes in the moment, no matter if it's a positive or negative one, and that is going to help them feel like they're being taken care of.

USE AN APPROPRIATE TONE OF VOICE

Your tone of voice also impacts the rapport you create with customers. Begin by meeting your customer wherever her energy is. If she's soft-spoken, don't get in her face. Likewise, if she is high energy, don't bring her down with a low-energy tone in your voice.

Ultimately, your tone of voice can even change the meaning of your words without you even knowing it if you are not intentional about your tone. If you don't want your customers having experiences like Anjelah Johnson spoofs via her Bon Qui Qui character, I recommend role playing with team members until you all learn how to adapt your tone to the situation while always keeping it positive and courteous.

BE HELPFUL

It may seem obvious to ensure your customers know you can help them by phrases such as, "I can help you with that" or, "Let me find out for you." Unfortunately, that is not what happens every day in small business.

To show the power in committing to results versus passing the buck, here are two ways to essentially say the same thing. Pay attention to how each of these makes you feel from the perspective of a customer:

Option 1
"Oh, John handles that and he's not here today. Hold on and I'll put you through to his voicemail."

Option 2
"I can help you with that. Let me connect you with John, who has your solution."

In Option 1, the person did not own the problem on behalf of the company. It basically told the customer their problem was not important that day and she'd have to wait. In Option 2, the employee presented herself as a problem solver, even though she still had to ultimately route her customer to John's voicemail.

The difference is how the customer is made to feel. Not every employee you hire will be a natural wordsmith, but every employee can learn to say, "I can help you with that" before deciding what path to take next.

Likewise, don't let your team members say, "I don't have the authority to do that." They have the authority to do anything that needs to happen by way of the resources (people and processes) you've provided them. Now, they might not be able to make a final decision without a manager, but they have the authority to go get the solution.

For example, Pam's customer says, "I demand a refund," and then Pam says, "Well, I don't have the authority to do that." Pam has just diminished the power she holds to handle this customer service crisis.

Wonk, wonk.

You want Pam to say, "I understand you would like a refund. Please excuse me for a moment while I speak to my manager to get her involved in your solution."

Remember, whether it's you or one of your employees, the person speaking with the customer is the messenger of your company. Empower your team by explaining that while they may not ultimately have the authority to make a final decision, they are still are the conduits to solutions.

LISTEN

Ask open-ended question so you can read between the lines to unveil what your customer wants and needs.

Repeat back the details and the desired end result to ensure everyone is on the same page, which then affords you the ability to meet your customer's expectations. In the same way, if your business fell short, repeat back everything your customer was dissatisfied with so they know you understand what their issue is and they feel heard and understood.

Important: don't interrupt. I know you're thinking about what you want to say next, but nothing will destroy a sale or escalate a problem faster than making a customer or potential customer feel unheard. If they want to tell you about their life aspirations and what type of customer experience they want to have, listen to them and mirror back what they told you so there is no question that they have been heard. That will get you further than any discount or refund ever could.

WORK WITH FACTS, NOT ASSUMPTIONS

Never assume anything about the customer, an employee, a business partner, or whoever's involved with customer experiences. Approach every day with curiosity, ask questions, and have your facts straight before taking action in response to customer feedback.

APOLOGIZE SINCERELY AND STRATEGICALLY

Even if the customer problem was not your or your company's fault, apologizing defuses the situation straight away.

Ways to apologize neutrally without accepting blame include:

"I'm so sorry to hear that."

"I'm sorry that we've disappointed you."

"I'm sorry you were inconvenienced."

Again, whether a customer missed her scheduled appointment, bought the wrong dress size, did not turn in a legal document by a deadline, or any myriad of customer-created problems, you still want to remain in the role of problem solver.

Follow up your neutral apology with this question: "What can I do to help?"

Bam. You are back in the driver's seat and now able to transform vent sessions into solutions.

AVOID TALKING SHOP

Don't displace blame by talking shop. Nobody cares that somebody called in sick, one of your computer systems is down, or you had more people order the special than usual, leaving you out of what they wanted to order for dinner. They just want what they paid for. Skip the long-winded story, apologize for their inconvenience, and then give customers options that actually are possible, even if that is picking a time the next day for you to follow up with them.

DON'T TAKE COMPLAINTS PERSONALLY

Remove emotion from your side of the equation as you consider your customer's emotions. Acknowledge that they're angry, hurt, disappointed, or whatever the emotions are on their end, and then know it's your job to come up with a solution. You just can't get butt-hurt over every customer complaint. Becoming emotional yourself in an already emotional situation only escalates the problem. Your customer is disappointed with her experience; she's not hating on you as a person. Whether or not it is valid, learn from the experience and then be sure to solve the problem your customer paid for. After all, that's what we defined business as in the Bombshell Business Dictionary.

Bombshell Quick Tip

If things escalate and your customer becomes irrational, first try to talk her off that ledge and get her to calm down by using a quieter voice yourself. Most hot-tempered people will take the cue and dial it down. However, never let a customer verbally abuse you or an employee. You can refuse service and even involve the appropriate authorities if the situation moves beyond your control.

TAKE A TIME-OUT

If you get dog-cussed by a customer, take a time-out before going back to your employees or before you deal with another customer who is happy and doesn't have any problems with you. For example, step outside for a moment or take three very deep breaths. Think about why you're in business. Think about all the marvelous customers you have who are happy with you. Think about all the problems you solve for those customers every day and how purposeful this makes you feel. Think about the happy work environment you have. Reset your mental game before you start dealing with other customers so you can shine brightly for them.

ENSURE SATISFACTION

Even when everything is going perfectly, go the next step to ensure your customer is completely satisfied.

You might say, "Mrs. Smith, thank you for giving me the opportunity to assist you today. Is there anything else I can help you with?"

Because what if there's something more? What if they need that prompt to remind them they planned to ask about gift certificates or operating hours on the weekend? Always offer the opportunity to assist your customer further; it builds an even stronger relationship.

NEVER FORGET THOSE WAGONS AND BUCKETS

With these tips, no matter how full your customer's wagon of experiences is or how much they want you to fill their bucket of expectations, you'll be able to meet your customer where she is, and train your team to do the same.

Take Action, Bombshell!

Visit www.thebombshellbusinesswoman.com for free, downloadable worksheets and resources.

1. *List your top three customer service challenges.*

2. *Based on what you learned in this chapter, how will you handle those challenges moving forward?*

3. *Create a quick script for each customer service challenge that you and your team members can effortlessly say, even when it's an uncomfortable situation.*

Seventeen

How to Hire and Inspire a Team

As I work with various brick-and-mortar businesses, I realize there is a common frustration when seeking advice about
building teams. Many female business personalities focus
their information toward online businesses that hire virtual,
contracted teams. Or they speak to solopreneurs who work
out of their home. If you have an online or home-based business, I encourage you to read this chapter all the same because
many parts of it are still applicable to you.

But what about the countless women who already have the
burden of a lease, utility bills, signage, and more, and then
have to take a calculated financial risk on top of everything
else each time she hires a new employee? This chapter is dedicated to you, Sister. Buckle up.

GETTING READY TO EXPAND

When should you hire your first employee? First, be sure
you want the responsibility. Never take lightly that becoming
an employer puts another person's ability to provide for their

life in your hands. These people will count on your business to earn a way to pay their bills, so be certain this is a responsibility you are willing to take on. Additionally, it puts you in a position of leadership. Leading another person professionally goes far beyond teaching someone how to do their job. How you to treat your employees at work has a rippling effect on how they treat their families and members of their communities.

Next, ensure your business—not just your druthers—demands it. Are you up to your eyeballs and constantly think, *I need another me?* Perfect. It's probably a good time to pass some of that work on to another person.

Then, be sure your business can afford it. If you are turning away business, you are likely in a position to hire. Further, if you have a new revenue stream you can viably pursue with additional help, then you could be ready to hire. Just don't forget that a salary is not the only expense associated with a new position. Other factors include taxes, benefits, bonuses, uniforms, supplies, equipment, and any myriad of expenses you may incur to keep a new employee operable and engaged.

If the time is now to hire your first employee, visit the Small Business Administration website to study up on the exact requirements that the government expects of you as an employer so you are fair, square, and legal. These include:

- How to obtain an Employer Identification Number (EIN) so you can properly report taxes and employee information to state agencies
- How to set up tax withholding records such as federal income tax, a federal wage and tax statement, and state taxes

- How to ensure your employee is legally allowed to work in the US

- How to properly notify your state about your new hires

- What you need to do to stay compliant with workman's comp insurance, labor laws, and tax reporting

FINDING THE RIGHT EMPLOYEE

Whether you are hiring your first employee or adding to the team, there are tried and true ways to find that next superstar for your business.

Begin by creating a thorough job description. The clearer you can be on what you expect in experience and job duties, the easier it will be to weed out those who are not a good fit. Be clear on the types of tools the person who holds this position will use, and if there are specific skill sets that are required, don't be shy about sharing that information.

To hire the best fit, the best way to find her or him is by referral. So start asking friends who know your personality and business who they might know for the role, and share your job description to be extra clear. Ask fellow members of associations and professional organizations to keep you in mind as they come across job seekers, as well as your alumni association, if applicable. Even better, set up a referral reward for your existing employees. No one is going to recruit a better fit than the people who have to work with this person every day and know your company's culture! That's why paying a bonus to employees who refer great employees to you after their referral has passed the sixty-day mark is financially advantageous. After all, replacing an employee costs 20 percent of that position's salary. If you compare that, or even the cost to advertise the position, to a $100 referral bonus, I'd say you are still winning in the financial and "best fit" department!

Take it a step further and post your job opening on your company's social media and your personal social media. Search LinkedIn for potential candidates and reach out to them directly.

Keep your eyes open, always. I may or may not be known for spotting talent in the most unlikely places, then recruiting people who weren't even looking for a new job to another company. When the culture fit is obvious and the service is great, I have no shame asking for a card or even going back to talk about potential opportunities.

You can post on online job sites if you need to cast a wider net. However, most of the time a small business will struggle to wade through the overwhelming number of unqualified candidates to get to the few who are viable for a first interview. Old-school methods are generally a better path for a small shop.

Of course, if you prefer a virtual team member on a contract basis or even part-time or full-time, you can turn to sites like Upwork or Fiverr to find talent worldwide. There are countless virtual staffing firms who can help you recruit a virtual team member in exchange for a small fee on the front end and an ongoing fee added to your monthly bill. A benefit of using a third party is that you don't actually enter an employer-employee relationship, and this might be appealing to someone who is not ready to take on the full responsibility of an employee yet needs help with their workload.

BOMBSHELL INTERVIEWING

Once you've found viable candidates, you'll want to take each applicant through a proper interview process. Create a standard interview process that includes:

- Situational "How would you handle it if _____?" types of questions so you can determine if her personal culture aligns with your company culture

- Questions about personality and conflict
- Questions about specific experiences
- Questions that show they can perform the job duties you need them to execute
- Checking references—*always*
- Hosting team interviews, then debriefing with your team to pull in what they think

MAKING THE OFFER

Make it special! You've just proposed to your new employee! Whether you type up an encouraging offer letter or send a gift to share your interest in hiring her or him, make their first moment with you memorable. They'll immediately feel their value and be excited to start working toward your objectives.

ONBOARDING AND TRAINING A NEW EMPLOYEE

Small business owners tend to skip several vital onboarding steps to get their new employees up and running and functional, filling in that ginormous gap that you have been so eager to deal with.

You might think:

Oh, we're just small mom and pop.

We're so small we just kind of wing it.

I'm here to tell you that the long-term impact and, specifically, positive financial impact, is much greater if you simply start off on the right foot with your new employees.

Don't take my word for it. According to The Society for Human Resource Management, new employees who participated in a well laid-out orientation program were 69 percent more likely to remain at a company up to three years.[1]

Let me say that again: 69 percent more likely to succeed if you just onboard them correctly!

Further, companies who have solid onboarding processes have new hires with a 54 percent greater productivity rate and a 50 percent greater new hire retention rate.[2]

I mean, hello.

Don't you want them to really dive in and get started? That's why you're just shoving them out into your business without properly training them, because you so desperately want them to pick up the slack. However, if you will just slow down and properly go through the five steps I outline in this chapter, they will be 54 percent more productive and 50 percent more likely to stick with you so you don't have to go through this entire process all over again!

Now, I know what you're thinking: *Oh, these are big corporate figures.*

But they are not, my friend. They are specific to small businesses. In fact, a CBS MoneyWatch report said that the cost of turnover, on the conservative side of things, is about 20 percent of an employee's annual earnings.[3]

Think about whatever position you're hiring for and write down the annual salary you plan to pay that person. Now write down 20 percent of that figure. That's the cost of your new hire leaving you and getting somebody else onboard to replace her or him. So let's do it right the first time, shall we?

Let's go through the steps of onboarding a new employee.

WELCOMING YOUR NEW EMPLOYEE

Identify Where Your New Employee Fits in the Mix

Give your new team member a personality assessment so you can see how they fit into the team dynamics. There are plenty of free options available if paid options are not quite in the budget. You can Google "free personality assessment" or visit www.thebombshellbusinesswoman.com to get links to those I recommend.

When you acknowledge and explore your new employee's unique characteristics, you welcome her into a bigger picture, showing her how she fits into something larger than herself. Meanwhile, you show the rest of your team how new team members will integrate into the existing team.

Complete the "Official Stuff"

Sit down with your new team member and be prepared with a packet of the essentials to complete. If you work remotely, this may look like attachments via email or even online forms. Don't let this linger over weeks and weeks saying, "Oh, yeah. I forgot to have you sign this. Oh, yeah, here's our insurance. Oh, yeah . . ."

Again, is that the customer experience you want? No? Then don't let your employee experience that, either.

In your packet include company standards, your legal and tax documents, insurance enrollment, whether you have full insurance or access to a supplemental policy, etc.

Then give them a tour of the work environment, and I say this every time—I am not kidding: don't forget the bathroom. There is nothing worse than having to ask, "Where can I go relieve myself?"

Show them around, tell them where they should park, and where they can store their lunch. Tell them where the AED device or fire extinguisher is, and the like. Prepare them for emergencies and make them feel at home so they don't have to feel as nervous as they already do. They're already going to be anxious about important things that come along with adapting to a new job. Don't make them stress over where they're supposed to put their lunch, OK?

Provide Access

Next, you need to provide your new employee with needed access. This also seems obvious, but even I have gone to work for weeks in a lead communication role with no access to email! (True story.) If your new employee can't login to your software, then they're not going to be very productive. Here's a checklist of accessibility you may need to provide for your new team member:

- A phone and email list of key employees, relevant vendors, emergency contacts, and anyone else they are going to interact with on a regular basis based on their job description, including who to call in an emergency

- Keys, pass cards, and/or passwords (ensuring they sign a document so you know who has keys and passwords to what)

- Uniforms or a dress code

- Access to shared calendars, folders, or files

- Authorization to make purchases on behalf of your company, such as access to a company credit card if they're eligible

- Association credentials

If you have the ability to add people to an association membership, leverage that account so your team member can learn more, take advantage of trainings and conferences, and achieve access to industry peers for best practices.

And, depending on the size of your business, you might want provide a map of the property or office space. You want them to know where everything is: their work station, the bathroom, the break room, emergency exits, and all the features that customers would be interested in.

Provide Tools and Resources

Ensure you hand over electronics, software, or any practical supplies an employee needs, like office supplies or even cleaning supplies.

A common mistake I see Bombshells make is categorizing team members as contractors but treating them like employees. There are several differentiating factors between the two, including behavioral, financial, and consideration of the type of relationship that exists.

The difference in the two determines who is responsible for providing equipment, such as a cell phone and data plan, a computer and Internet access, job-related supplies (such as products for an aesthetician or hairdresser), and more.

According to the IRS, "If you classify an employee as an independent contractor and you have no reasonable basis for doing so, you may be held liable for employment taxes for that worker."[4]

Provide Proper Training

Train your new employee properly. Sounds so obvious, and yet it often doesn't happen. Create a training plan that is mapped out day by day.

Provide an employee manual where the basics can be found. Your written company culture, company policies, holidays (the days that you're closed and/or paid holidays), benefit information, available perks, and your company history. Tell them about the why and how. How did all this start? Why does it matter? How do they fit into that history? How do they fit into the future?

Then provide thorough, job-specific training: what

processes to use, how to use equipment, how to respond to common customer questions, and more.

Then, of course, the last thing you want to do when you're in training mode with your new employee is confirm understanding of job expectations. Do they know what it is they're supposed to do? Have they thoroughly read their job description? Do they have any questions about it? Is there anything they would like to add to it that they think they can do more of, or better, or something that perhaps you didn't talk about in the interview process that suddenly caught them off guard, or that you have changed your mind about?

Set Expectations

You want to talk to your newest team member about their individual goals and the employee review process. They need to understand now, at the get-go, what they're going to be measured on, how that process works, and what they can expect in the future so they know how it will go when they are evaluated. It helps them start living up to the bar you set for them and removes the anxiety of trying to figure out if they are meeting expectations.

Commit to Regular Check-Ins

Once you set job expectations, talk about individual goals, the employee review process, and how the review process works.

Always encourage an open-door policy. Don't let that be lip service. Make sure you tell team members that if something doesn't feel right, they should come to you so it can be quickly and efficiently resolved. That requires you to have an open mind, an open heart, and so, genuinely, an open door.

Of course, as they are getting their feet wet in their new job, you want to give immediate feedback, both positive and negative. If they did a really great job or they caught onto something super quickly, tell them then and there while you're in the moment.

Then you want to conduct a one-on-one thirty-day check-in. Ask how things are going and if there's anything they need. Do they believe they need any tools and resources you haven't provided for them? How are they getting along with everybody? Do they feel they're getting comfortable in their position and moving forward toward their goals? Simple questions. It doesn't have to be super formal.

Then, of course, you want to do a sixty-day check-in as well. Note this: at sixty days, your new employee is at the highest risk time for turnover. They've gotten over the honeymoon phase, and now they're really getting into the business of doing business. If things aren't clicking for them, this is when they're talking to themselves, saying things like, *Oh, did I make the right decision?* Or, *Maybe I could be making more money somewhere else.* Or, *I'm very frustrated. I'm not catching on. If I don't catch on soon, I'm probably going to get hacked anyway.*

You want to be sure, at that sixty-day point, that you are on the same page as your employee.

If something's not clicking, then you need to have an open, honest conversation about it. Likewise, if it's not working on your end, that's probably a good time to cut ties so you're not getting deeper into a situation you can't get yourself out of so they're not doing damage to your business, your brand, your reputation, your company culture. If it's not working out by sixty days, if both sides aren't singing "Kumbaya," that's a good time for either side to say, "OK, we thought this was a good plan, but it's not." Hopefully, you did your homework by properly sourcing your candidates, asking all the right questions, and onboarding them effectively . . . but sometimes things happen, and that's OK too. We prefer for them not to, but if it happens, sixty days is probably a good time to sever that tie respectfully.

PLANNING FOR THE FUTURE

Even if you're not ready to hire somebody right now, take some time to map these things out so you don't have to while you're in the weeds.

Get ready to take action, Bombshell, employer of other human beings who depend on you for them to pay their bills! This is the time to be a big girl. This is the time to take your business seriously and stop saying, as I've heard so many times, "Oh well, we're real relaxed. We're, like, really chill here."

That's not the behavior of a Bombshell Business Woman. I want you to take the viability and leadership of your employees seriously. Treat your employees like you would want to be treated if you were an employee. It all starts with a plan. But of course, you know I'm going to say that because I'm Amber, and I plan!

Take Action, Bombshell!

Visit www.thebombshellbusinesswoman.com for free, downloadable worksheets and resources.

1. *Write down which personality assessment you will use for new employees.*

2. *List the legal and official documents you need your new employee to complete immediately upon hiring.*

3. *List the access you need to grant to a new employee.* (Remember, some access is job specific.)

4. *List the tools and resources your new employee will need.*

(This is also job specific.)

5. *Write down what your new employee will learn each day of their first week or two, as well as who will train them in each area of their responsibilities.*

6. *Create goals for your new employee that you can use to measure their performance.*

Eighteen

Using Technology: Teaching Wilma Flintstone in a Jane Jetson World

I pick my technology like I picked my husband. It has to complement, not complicate, my life. While I understand that technology can be one of the most intimidating parts of small business, it also has the power to streamline, simplify, and automate processes that would otherwise suck valuable time from your life.

In this chapter, I will show you how to succeed as a Stone Age Wilma from *The Flintstones* in a futuristic business world—think Jane Jetson of *The Jetsons*.

If you want to get out of and stay out of the weeds, check out my recommended resources in the Bombshell Business Tech Toolbox. Links to the various websites can be found at www.thebombshellbusinesswoman.com.

BUSINESS SYSTEMS

G Suite by Google Cloud

Get a professional, legitimate-looking email (you@ yourcompany.com vs. yourcompany@gmail.com), cloud storage, collaboration, and admin tools, as well as 24-7 customer support. Consider it your small business's own fancy-schmancy enterprise system like the big guys have, only you pay next to nothing. I could not run my business without this.

Google Drive

Get access to files anywhere through secure cloud storage and file backup for your photos, videos, files, and more. It's like the Microsoft Office Suite of programs (Word, Excel, PowerPoint, etc.) only in the cloud. Plus, there are more tools and the ability to collaborate with others in real time on the same document. This is part of G Suite, but you also automatically get a free Google Drive if you have a free Gmail account. I personally live in Google Drive to the point people tease me about it!

DropBox

Dropbox is a free service that lets you bring all your photos, docs, and videos anywhere. If you need to share a really ginormous file that won't send as an attachment or if you don't want to store huge files on your hard drive, this is a must-have resource.

Evernote

There isn't enough space to describe Evernote. You can store files, ideas, web clippings—anything—in organized folders to reference later or to collaborate with others. I look at it as a dashboard for projects in motion.

INBOX MANAGEMENT

Unroll.me

When I enrolled in this super amazing (free) service it immediately picked up all my email subscriptions, which—no surprise—alerted me that I had *way* too many. Too many in spite of the fact that I dutifully unsubscribe manually as often as possible.

There is just no way to keep up. Some subscriptions I legitimately want and I don't mind their frequency or time of day that they come in. Most, however, have infiltrated my inbox in some covert way, and no matter how many times I try to boot 'em, I still have them.

No mas!

That's right, one simple enrollment process and all I had to do was one of three things while scrolling through this list:

1. Click unsubscribe. And let me tell ya, that felt good.

2. Add the subscription to my daily Rollup—meaning every day I can pick what time I receive this *one* email featuring all my subscriptions from that day, and then I can decide which ones I feel like reading. In. The. Driver's. Seat. *Boom.* Once reviewing them in my daily Rollup, I can hit Unsubscribe to any of them if I decide I really don't want it at all or I can even release it back into the wild of my inbox.

3. Do nothing. Those subscriptions will still appear in my inbox based on the senders' timeline and frequency.

The first time I did this, I unsubscribed to 65 noisy, annoying emails that meant nothing to me and "rolled up" an additional 49. And then the hallelujah angels sang—and I felt like I had punched those pesky emails in the face! (You'll see . . . it just feels that good.)

Of course, if you are about to go to Sephora, Bed Bath and Beyond, or Home Depot and want to see if you happened to get a coupon emailed to you, you don't have to wait for your Rollup to arrive in your inbox for the day. You can just log on to Unroll.me and get right to those emails that are hanging out, out of your way on the Unroll.me website. No big deal.

Boomerang

This also free, handy-dandy tool is ahh-may-zing. It's no secret that I am *totally* against allowing your inbox to dictate your day's priorities, and this little tool helps you postpone your knee-jerk reaction by sending that email back to you later when you know you'll have time to address it. It is simply insurance for epic brain farts, forgetfulness, and email overwhelm.

You can even have Boomerang mark each message you do this to as unread, or you can label or star them. What's more, it can also send emails in the future for those occasions you want to send an email while you are thinking about it, but want your recipient to receive it when they are most likely to react to it. You don't have to be logged in to your email account or even have your computer on for this to happen, either. What? True story.

WEBSITE PLATFORM

WordPress

Due to its ability to endlessly customize to meet my needs, WordPress is my preferred website platform. It has robust features, is fairly easy to use (although beginners need to get familiar with its options), and is used by mega brands. Originally known for bloggers, all types of businesses quickly caught on that a highly professional website can be created on WordPress, and it is now the dominant player in the game. Best of all, with super affordable hosting from a provider like Go Daddy or Bluehost, you can create a website on the cheap with thousands of their free templates and even more free plug-ins that can customize your site to fit the needs of your customers and prospects.

Other Platforms

There are alternatives like Squarespace, Wix, and Weebly, but if you want your website to be able to grow with you while containing your costs and expanding your options, my resident experts all agree that WordPress is the way to go.

CUSTOMER RELATIONSHIP AND PROJECT MANAGEMENT

Insightly

This is a simple to use yet powerful CRM system for small business that helps manage your contacts from leads to vendors and even suppliers, as well as your email history, projects, and events. Its reports help you stay on top of your business and conversions. It also has a widget that allows you to convert any email into a task and even assign it to another team member *right in the email itself.* Truly, what more could you ask for? Well, an app or a free version, but they have you covered there too.

Asana

Asana is a project management software that affords project and task management and facilitates team communication and collaboration. This eliminates the need for email and third-party apps, even when working with people outside your organization. You can share projects, assign tasks, share files, and leave comments all in one place. Asana is free, with premium and enterprise versions available.

FINANCIAL TECH TOOLS

Freshbooks

If I didn't have this prebookkeeper, I would have epically failed at accounting. Not only does Freshbooks produce professional invoices and accept payments, it can automatically populate your expenses from your business bank account(s), track time connected to a project, and it's *crazy easy* to use. It even has an app that allows you to take pictures of your receipts and record expenses that way too. More geared towards freelancers and service providers, it is also limited on reporting and is difficult to move into a larger platform. However, it is the easy button and, in my humble opinion, the best place to start to keep your financial poop in a group. Plus, they have multiple app integrations and award-winning customer service, which I will personally vouch for. Love me some Freshbooks.

Xero

Like its main competitor, Quickbooks, Xero does all the things you would expect of an accounting software, such as online accounting, invoicing, billing, and banking. However, Xero flexes its muscles uniquely by allowing you to monitor your real-time cash flow, keeping track of transactions on the go via its slick app. Xero also allows for unlimited users, no matter what your subscription plan, whereas QuickBooks Online limits your users, depending on the size of your plan. If you're like me and you need the user interface to be "pretty," Xero is the more user-friendly option over Quickbooks. Also notable for customer service and integrations with other apps, Xero is a snazzy answer for your small business accounting needs.

PayPal

From accepting credit cards on a website to online invoicing, you can easily manage all your business payment needs with PayPal's merchant services. I like this option over Square or others because it is FDIC-insured and *far* more secure with people's banking information. My banking friends give PayPal two thumbs up, so that's good enough for me!

Stripe

Geared toward online businesses, and super user-friendly, Stripe can store card information, process subscriptions, power marketplaces, and more. Stripe strives to be flexible for Internet commerce opportunities, whether you create a subscription service, an on-demand marketplace, an e-commerce store, or a crowdfunding platform.

EMAIL MARKETING

ConvertKit

ConvertKit was created specifically for bloggers, but it is a powerful tool for any business that wants to easily manage emails lists and drip campaigns based on customer interests. Not only is it SUPER easy to use and moderately priced, the interface is lovely and inviting and you can even *resend* an email only to those who didn't open your email with one click of a button. I cannot brag on this company enough, from the culture to the die-hard commitment to creating an affordable product that truly meets the needs of its customers without overcomplicating things. I *heart* ConvertKit!

Infusionsoft

Infusionsoft is for a business that desires to map out and automate each step of the sales and marketing strategy. It can help sales team members nurture leads and scale personal relationships with customers. Like ConvertKit, but perhaps with a bit more sophistication, Infusionsoft allows you to "tag" leads and customers. This then automates the sales funnels your customers should go through based on their interests and actions. This is what you move up to when you're ready to stop doing so much manual work with your segmented email lists. It is costlier and what I would consider an advanced tool.

Mailchimp

This is a beautiful, fun online email marketing solution to manage contacts, send emails, and track results. If you need an attractive user interface and a no-brainer solution to send newsletters and sales emails, this is it. I love Mailchimp for early beginnings before you learn about the real power in email marketing and want the features to back that up. There is a free version and then super affordable packages you can upgrade to as you grow.

Aweber

Aweber is a more powerful tool than Mailchimp and allows you to better segment your lists and track affiliate sales. Oh, and I should mention it has amazing customer service. You can even call them! You read that right. The user interface isn't as "pretty" as Mailchimp, no monkey is going to high-five you when you successfully send a broadcast (like in Mailchimp), nor are the features as robust as Infusionsoft; however, it is the perfect solution if you want to get started right (and don't "need" pretty like me) or if you need a next step up from Mailchimp.

SALES TOOLS

Leadpages

Leadpages helps you create landing pages that are optimized and mobile-responsive. With templates and a drag-and-drop interface, Leadpages is the easy button for creating pages to build your email list, sell products and services, and more. It integrates well with WordPress, making it appear as if it is native to your website.

Shopify

Shopify was created to support online stores. You can customize your storefront, organize and sell your products, track and respond to orders, and accept credit cards—all in one world. I see many Bombshells using various tools to create a feasible solution for their online store. Shopify is the one-stop "shop" solution (pun intended).

CREATIVE/PRODUCTION

Canva

Canva makes design simple for everyone. Yes, everyone includes you. You can create designs for Web or print: blog graphics, presentations, Facebook covers, flyers, posters, invitations, and more. It is absolutely free, but the pro version allows you to upload your brand fonts, create brand templates, create color themes for your brand, and more to make your visual brand game an easy one-two play. This could be the number one favorite tool of Bombshells. As an avid user, I've served in an advisory capacity and have beta tested nearly every new feature since they came on the scene. I can personally speak to their sincere interest in providing a tool that meets their customers' highest needs.

Adobe Creative Cloud

If you have some design, movie, or audio editing experience or are taking courses to help you learn this "for realies" software, then this is the ticket. It is the more advanced software I learned in college on route to my PR degree and what the pros use. Since the suite's graphic design software take more steps than I often have time for, I lean heavily on Canva for my day-to-day use. There is no doubt, though, that Adobe's technology will provide a higher-quality end product.

Jing

This handy plug-in captures anything you see on your computer screen, as an image or short video, and then lets you share it instantly. And it's free. I use it daily to communicate with team members, clients, vendors, and peers. If a picture is worth a thousand words, then this tool is your new jam.

Screenflow (for Mac)

With Screenflow you can record the contents of your entire monitor while also capturing your video camera, iOS device, microphone, and computer audio. I use this to record training presentations and edit video. This is an ideal software to create training videos for your team from company culture presentations to technical or even customer service training.

Camtasia (for Mac or PC)

Camtasia is like Screenflow. While I did test-drive Camtasia, which is also easy to use and available for PC, I ultimately thought Screenflow was more intuitive. However, it also gives you the tools you need to record on-screen activity, edit and enhance your content, and share in high quality to viewers anywhere.

VIRTUAL HELP

Upwork

Sometimes you need a little extra help, but you can't bring on a new team member. Or perhaps the help you need is project-based with a start and end in mind. That's when you should consider using a site like Upwork.com. Formerly Elance-oDesk, Upwork is a global freelancing platform where businesses and independent professionals connect and collaborate remotely. You can find just about any type of service you may need by posting a job and taking applications from various vendors worldwide. You can also approach a specific user to apply for a job. The best part is that you pay for your work through Upwork, which protects you from fraud or even plain ol' poor service.

Fiverr

Known for its $5 gigs, you can find vendors to create graphics, marketing materials, transcription services, video services, and more with specific turnaround times in mind. "Gigs" start at $5, but can quickly increase in price, so be careful that you don't overspend by selecting too many add-on services. This is one of those sites that makes me say, "I love the Internet!"

BONUS TOOLS

LastPass

Only remember one password—your LastPass master password. Save all your usernames and passwords to LastPass, and it will automatically log in to your sites and sync your passwords everywhere you need them. In fact, you can have a super complicated, unique, hacker-proof password for every site you visit because LastPass will create it for you. Stop the insanity, for real.

CamScanner App

Need to scan and send something like right now? Grab your phone, open your CamScanner app, snap a photo (or multiple photos if you are "scanning" a multipage document) and watch CamScanner clarify the image and convert it into a PDF that is ready to share with anyone digitally. Viola. Who makes this stuff up, anyway? Whoever you are, I love you.

Bombshell Quick Tip

If you have techphobia, I recommend starting with a tool that addresses your greatest pain point right now. Once you master that first tool and experience how technology can streamline your operations, add another and then another. Before you know it, you'll be like many "Wilma" Bombshells who came before you who abandoned their notepads and sticky notes in favor of a more "Jane-style" approach to business.

Take Action, Bombshell!

Visit www.thebombshellbusinesswoman.com for free, downloadable worksheets and resources.

1. *List your top three pain points.*

2. *Choose a tech tool per pain point that will help ease the business drama.*

3. *Now, Wilma, write down why it is important to stick it out through the learning curve for these tools. Come back to this statement as many times as you need to until you've mastered each tool.*

Nineteen

Applying Time Strategy

Now it's time to stop talking about your dreams and actually turn them into reality. You've discovered how to understand yourself both as an individual and as a visionary leader of your business brand, but where the rubber really meets the road is the actual execution in the day-to-day of your business.

I hear you grumbling. I know this is not the fun part, but what is fun is success. So we have to take the small steps, each day, to get there. Yes, this is this point where other experts start talking about time management, but I am here to tell you that time management is a myth.

Time cannot be managed. It's going to pass you by, whether or not you are trying to manage it. If you are not spending your time doing what is going to move your business forward by fulfilling your Business Mojo, time doesn't care. It's just going to blow on by, anyway.

What I'd like to do instead is talk about time strategy. What is possible is looking at the available time that you have before you, and then strategically coming up with ways you can capitalize on that time for its highest use.

When I think of time management, I think of the story of the little Dutch boy on his way to school who was passing the dyke that had sprung a leak. He stuck his little finger in it to try to prevent the ocean from flooding his town. There is no way in the world he could have continued to effectively prevent the dike from bursting simply by reacting to each leak that sprung. A proactive plan, however, could have saved this weary little boy from his tiresome and ultimately fruitless efforts.

Time management is reactive, whereas time strategy is proactive. Time strategy requires you to think like an engineer: someone who comes in, assesses the situation, determines what processes need to be followed, what contractors need to be involved, and who knows how to motivate everyone to complete the project on time and with excellence.

Personally, I'd rather be the engineer than the little Dutch boy.

So where do we start? I believe if we can be as strategic as possible where we spend the majority of our time, which is in our professional life, we can then make strides in our personal life, and then ultimately (gasp) have time to focus on ourselves.

We can talk about hiring the right team members and outsourcing, but the true reality is that even with help, we are still going to find ways to overwhelm ourselves, as well as overcommit and overpromise our time. Without a plan, it's hard to break this cycle.

Now, I know. You dream every day. You have big visions for what you could do . . . one day.

I'm here to tell you, though, that it takes as much energy to wish as it does to plan, and as entrepreneurs, we tend to be dreamers. The problem is, if you can't ever realize your dreams because you haven't created a road map, then you start to have that soul-crushing experience so many female entrepreneurs fall prey to.

Maybe you start telling yourself, *It's never going to happen,* or, *I am slave to my business,* or, *I am just not cut out for this. Maybe I just need to get a job.*

It doesn't have to feel that way.

The fact of the matter is, every minute you spend planning, you save ten minutes in execution. That's huge. So if you want nine minutes of your life back, this is a very easy way to do it.

I am all about preparation because I have ADD. For the longest time, it was such a dark, dirty secret until I realized what it was in my early twenties, and how I could leverage it as a strength, rather than succumbing to the challenges I faced as a highly driven professional with Attention Deficit Disorder. Frankly, I don't even know why they call it a disorder. It's really a superpower.

I love, love, love—*love* to plan. Frankly, I am like that person who lost a hundred pounds and then suddenly wants everyone around me to eat tofu. I was always a hot mess. I had amazing ideas, but I wasn't able to implement them, which is why I always felt like a failure. So after working with a counselor for years, reading up as much as possible on the subject, and being acutely aware of how I personally function (what motivates me, what I hate to do, what I love to do, when I need to borrow help, and all those kinds of things), I was able to develop systems that not only helped me, they also helped my employees, my friends, my mastermind clients, and more. In fact, these are the strategies I now teach people all over the world.

START TIME-BUCKETING

First, let's talk about time-bucketing. You can time-bucket

by day and you can time-bucket by the time of day. Now what does that look like?

Monday	Tuesday	Wednesday	Thursday	Friday
Content Creation	Client Work	Client Work	Client Work	Administrative Work

Let's look at my week so you have a concrete example. On Mondays, I don't take on clients. I just don't. That is the day I can focus on writing my content, creating content for paying clients, putting together presentations, or doing anything that's creative. I leave Mondays for that because I am rested from my weekend and my creative juices are more likely to flow.

Also, if I am traveling from a Friday to Monday, it's something I can do from anywhere and still not get behind. So I can plan to write as a passenger on an airplane or riding shotgun in the car, and know that that part of my work can still get done for the week. When it is done, I can then completely turn my attention to my clients. That means I don't have to shift between my strategic and process-oriented mind-set and my creative side throughout the day. Instead, I can be strategic and process-oriented when I am helping my clients, then be fully focused on the creative side of my business on the days where I carved out the time to remain in my flow.

So Mondays are typically my little golden day where I get to be my little creative self, which is truly at the core who I am. If you can carve out your golden day, golden half day, or even a golden hour, where you can work in your highest value, I strongly urge you to do that.

Tuesdays, Wednesdays, and Thursdays are reserved for clients, such as brand and leadership consulting, one-on-one coaching clients, corporate presentations, and more. For three days, I remain in the same mode, wear the same type of clothes, speak the same language, and live in a strategic problem-solving space. When I go to bed on those nights, I think about and pray over my clients. There is not a lot of room for my own business needs or creativity, but that's OK, because I handled that first on Monday, remember?

Yes, I put me first. You should try it sometime.

Now, remember, I am paper-certified ADD. By design, I have monkey mind. So, time-bucketing, and ensuring I have a day to dump out all my creativity first, allows me to focus on my clients and overdeliver my brand promise on my three client-focused days. The monkeys have been held at bay.

But the week's not over yet.

On Fridays, I focus on administrative processes and business operations like budgeting (yuck), paying and sending out invoices (double yuck), and that sort of thing. So it's a little bit of a catch-all day. Whatever I don't get done during the week, I have Friday to get it done. This enables me to stop my day at an appropriate time. I know I have time carved out for the inevitable catch-up.

I have scheduled margin into my workflow.

Not every business has the flexibility to assign days to specific functions, though. Many spas, boutiques, fitness centers, restaurants, and hotels have no choice but to blend customer service and operations into every day.

In that case, I encourage you to time-bucket parts of your day. For example, one of my clients does not engage with customers before 10 a.m. She does not touch email, talk to customers, respond to text messages, or do anything except for the work that she thinks needs to get done. She knocks out her behind-the-scenes work first thing in the morning, or she knows she will say yes to everything that comes her way, her agenda for the day will be hijacked, and the important but not urgent tasks she needs to accomplish to maintain a healthy business will come last . . . if she gets to them at all. With this wisdom, she always puts herself first.

I choose Mondays, my client chooses mornings, but we both put the business of doing business first, or else there will be no business to serve others.

Do you see the importance of this?

BATCH SIMILAR WORK

Another way of looking at this is time-bucketing your tasks. Some people refer to this as "batching your work." If you need to write a blog post for example, are you going to just write one blog post, or would it be wise to write all four weekly blogs for the month while you are already in the zone? Or how about recording videos for social media? If you are going to take out all the equipment to record videos, put on a full face of makeup, and have your hair all done, for heaven's sake, that's probably a good time to hammer out multiple videos. Just change your shirt, put your hair up versus down, swap out your earrings, and voila, no one knows the difference. It looks like you recorded them on different days.

Batching or "bucketing" your tasks is ripping the Band-Aid off whenever you have to deal with ongoing activities. I have found that most of the women I work with are like me and hate monotonous tasks and thrive on deadline. If you ask me (and you are because you are reading this book), sprinting through less than desirable tasks is far more enjoyable than running a marathon you're not really into anyway.

STAY IN THE ZONE

Bucketing your time or your tasks keeps you in the zone. Mondays are my creative zone. If that zone is disrupted, it's hard for me to get back in the zone. When you are invoicing, processing receipts, and living in your accounting software or bookkeeper's homework, you just get it all done at once and stay in a more analytical, focused zone.

Girl, save all of those receipts throughout the week and then record those expenses on Friday or whatever day you time-bucket or batch those type of activities. Don't make the suffering endure all week if you are like me and you hate dealing with numbers.

Bombshell Quick Tip

Brainstorm how you can time-bucket:

- What would your week look like?

- What would each day look like?

- Are your mornings different than your afternoons?

This is your business, so you define your workflow . . . and remember to put your business first!

MASTER THE WEEKLY CALENDAR BOOGIE

Raise your hand if your calendar ever makes you feel the need for an oxygen mask!

Yup, you're for sure a Bombshell! (Told you so!)

I call dealing with your calendar the "calendar boogie" because you seriously have to dance around to pull it all together. You have to go gather all the different information from various calendars, like your child's school or team calendars, your personal calendar, your business calendar, your project management deadlines, your volunteer or church calendars, your spouse's calendar, and more. With these obligations "out there," how do you figure out how to budget time with yourself?

I know you have many a time when you want to say, "Um, hi. I'm like trying to run a business here, in case no one was noticing."

. I see you, girl! And I have a working solution for you.

Step 1: Fill in Your Calendar

Every week, I want you to look ahead at the upcoming two weeks.

Wait, why two weeks, Amber? you ask.

Well, how many times have you transitioned into your next week and been caught with your pants down? It is like, *Oh my gosh! I didn't realize that was coming up. How did that happen so quickly?*

I mean, not to be the mistress of the obvious here, but it was probably on your calendar and you didn't look that far . . .

Awkward silence.

OK, so back to the "Every week, look at your next two weeks" thing.

On a routine day each week, ensure all your personal items are filled in first. This is so you can avoid forgetting your kid on a scheduled half day at school that you planned a meeting on.

Not that I've ever done that.

Step 2: List Your To-Dos

Now, make a list of the most important work-related projects for the week. See what meetings you might need to be prepared for; check what deadlines are approaching in the next two weeks on your project management spreadsheets or software. Then, prioritize and distribute those tasks to each work day. This makes you apply your bigger plans into tactical to-dos, day by day. Comparing your to-dos to your calendar helps you realistically project your bandwidth to accomplish operational tasks because you can actually see on your calendar how many appointments you have, what *type* of meetings and commitments you have, and ultimately what will be required of you to manage the things already demanding your time. Only then can you delegate your other tasks and hit your deadlines . . . and ultimately reach your goals and fulfill your dreams.

Yes, I'm telling you that responsibly applying time strategy and proactively leveraging your calendar is the dumb ol' secret to seeing your dreams come true.

I realize it's not a very sexy solution, but you can listen to motivational speakers, say mantras every morning when you wake, and pray until you're sanctified, but if you don't get to doing the work, it ain't gonna happen, Sister!

Bombshell Quick Tip

If your to-do will take less than 15 minutes, it's a task and can be added to a block of time scheduled to knock out small tasks.

If it takes more than 15 minutes, make an appointment on your calendar with yourself to get it done. What you think will take 15 minutes will likely take you 30 or more, so try to be honest with yourself.

If you were stranded in the ocean in a small boat with a paddle, I'd tell you to pray to God, but row for the shore! God has given you an intellect, gifts, and talents, along with tools and resources and the power to walk in His purpose. So get to walking, will ya? And while you're walking, to ensure you don't wander around aimlessly, empower yourself with your road map: your calendar and your to-dos.

It's just that boring and simple.

OK, now take a quick, deep breath. You have a lot of planning to do to be a true Bombshell, but if you just go through this process every week, you will be far less stressed.

Certainty breeds confidence, and that's what we're after, right?

PRIORITIZE DAILY TASKS

Last, I want to offer you a way to prioritize your daily tasks. I created this system after a highly intelligent and very accomplished client couldn't get in a good rhythm that worked for him after trying all different types of systems. I mean, we tried Steven Covey's system, the Getting Things Done system, and all types of systems, and it just wasn't working for his creative mind. No matter how much he planned to do something, he was always attracted to the creative tasks on his to-do list first. Then, he'd find himself in a mess when he did not attend to his analytical tasks. He was in full-on panic mode when deadlines loomed with consequences. It just wasn't fun. It wasn't fun for him and it wasn't fun for me as his coach because I was watching him drown.

So I developed a way for him to be real with his tendencies and the consequences of his decisions. Once I realized it worked for him, I started using it with other clients as well, creatives and noncreatives alike. It worked universally with success, so now you can give it a whirl yourself.

	Creative Tasks	Analytical Tasks
Urgent	1. 2. 3. 4. 5.	1. 2. 3. 4. 5.
Nice to Have Done	1. 2. 3. 4. 5.	1. 2. 3. 4. 5.

So, as you can see, the first row is for urgent tasks, which are deadline-oriented or have consequences if they don't get done.

On the left side, there is room for creative tasks. For example, a graphic designer might need to complete a design concept that she promised to a client that day. So that is both a time-sensitive and a creative task. That would go on the upper-left quadrant.

The right side of the top row, however, is for the analytical tasks that typically aren't popular with creatives. Creatives tend to procrastinate on tasks that require left-brain thinking because that's out of their comfort zone. However, if that graphic designer doesn't invoice the client for the work that was done, how will she stay in business? It has to get done, no matter if she gets warm fuzzies doing it or not.

This top row realistically reveals her top priorities of her day.

The bottom row features tasks that need to get done, but

could possibly get moved to another day of the week. For example, this same graphic designer might need to start an inspiration board on Pinterest for an upcoming project, which would be noted on the lower left side. Or she might need to record a few receipts to keep up with her expenses for the week—an analytical task. While those are both important tasks that keep her business moving forward, there are no real consequences if they aren't done that same day.

Of course, if she keeps pending those tasks to another day over and over again, they will very likely end up in that top row one day soon.

Do your best in the day, for the day, and then work on tomorrow when it comes. Show yourself grace and laugh at yourself. Be sure to ask for help, and vent or brag on your progress along the way. Remember, you are not aspiring for perfection, Bombshell. You are aspiring for progress, one step at a time.

Take Action, Bombshell!

Visit www.thebombshellbusinesswoman.com for free, downloadable worksheets and resources.

1. *Decide how you want to apply time-bucketing to your days or parts of your days.*

2. *Choose how to batch similar tasks each week, when possible.*

3. *Look two weeks ahead and assign to-dos for each day based on what's coming up on your calendar and your project plans.*

4. *Use my time strategy template (or whatever productivity system already works for you) to prioritize your tasks each day.*

Twenty

Embracing Your
Inner Bombshell

Girl, I'm going to hand it to you. Being a Bombshell Business Woman demands much from your mind, body, and spirit. Then add the fact that women keep a running tally in their head of everything and everybody they have to keep up with in addition to their business, and it's no wonder men think we are certifiably crazy!

I don't know about you, but at the end of the worst kind of days, I feel like a warrior who, despite the gut punches, setbacks, and daily scramble to make it all happen, finds a secret satisfaction in knowing I did, in fact, make it all happen.

On the good days, I'm humbled by being able to share my God-given gifts, energized that I can show His love through my work, and proud to be an example of His grace in action to my children and others.

So now I'm called. Called to tell you that you've so got this. I'm driven to share what I've overcome in life to get to where

I am today because I want you to believe that no matter what you've been through and no matter how challenging life or business is right now, you can choose to start making better decisions that will reroute the trajectory of your future.

And people are going to try to stop you because your success makes underachievers come face-to-face with their own inadequacies and sorry little lives. That has created an epidemic in this world where people simply don't feel empowered or confident enough to *step into their greatness* and play *big* in life. That's why I hear women say things like:

- "I didn't say anything in the meeting because I didn't want to be the dissenting voice."

- "I would step up and help lead, but I don't want to step on John's toes."

- "I wanted to get out there and dance, but didn't want to cause attention to myself."

My only natural response to such statements is, "Huh?!" Let me flip the script here and ask questions in return:

- What if other people thought the same as you, but were also too afraid to speak up, leaving the end result that everyone left agreeing to something only one person believed in?

- What if John desperately needs help, but doesn't know how to ask? Or what if you stepped in and your collaboration was transformational?

- What if by you going out on the dance floor, it broke the ice for everyone else at the party to do the same? What if fun was possible for all with your first dance?

Well, Bombshell, that nonsense talk ends now. You are now

a bold, brave, and unwaveringly confident fempreneur and that authority is going to spill over into all areas of your life.

I don't know how I—a short, redheaded, pale-complected, freckle-faced dreamer with ADD—managed to grow up with such acceptance of myself. I am not sure how being a highly visible leader in my high school only to end up "knocked up" at age sixteen didn't disarm me, but instead fueled my mission further. I wish I could come up with some recipe, because I could make millions selling it. I guess what I can boil it down to is my deeply embedded belief in the bolded phrase in the prominently displayed wall decal I have in my entryway, featuring an excerpt from Marianne Williamson's *A Return to Love: Reflections on the Principles of A Course in Miracles.*

Your playing small does not serve the world.

By *not* stepping into your greatness, you are letting down everyone around you whom you can inspire, touch, or influence. You see, it's really not about you. It's about everyone around you, so ditch the guilt and insecurity you have about "standing out."

How dare you not?

Truly—I know how you feel. I get it. You don't want to get those looks that I've received. You don't want people to say, "Well, she just wants attention" or, "She thinks highly of herself."

But I must ask: Who cares what insecure people think who are insanely jealous that you are OK with yourself?

Really?

Anyone who knows me or has worked with me knows I am very much a behind-the-scenes person who likes to make others shine. My greatest joy is in helping others be their best.

But how can I do that if people don't know me and what I stand for? If I don't step up as a leader? If I don't contribute to the conversation or get the party started so others can feel permission to do the same?

The small voices of small people who think small thoughts and live in their small worlds will never stop me from playing big and fulfilling my purpose . . . and I challenge you to *stick that thought in your pipe and smoke it* until you start feeling comfortable saying the same thing about your own life.

Much to the confusion of small-minded people, *confidence* does not equate *arrogance*. If you don't believe me, look those two words up in the dictionary!

Yes, things started out pretty shaky for me, and I haven't even divulged all that I could with you in fear of overwhelming you. Yet, now in my season of plenty, I can say that the very principles I shared with you in this book empowered me to do unimaginable things for a young mother starting out behind the eight ball.

But, I would not be properly wielding my velvet machete if I didn't address your buts.

I know, I can hear you saying it right now . . .

- But, sometimes what you ask me to do is just too hard.

- But, change is painful.

- But, I might actually have to do things that are uncomfortable for my personality. I am an introvert and you are asking me to network. I am extroverted and you are asking me to sit behind a computer and put processes together.

- But, I am not very consistent. What if I fail?

While those things all might be true, here's the cold hard truth.

Sitting still while a needle injects Botox® into your face

repeatedly is hard.

Childbirth and high heels are painful.

Smothering hot wax on your eyebrows and then ripping tiny hairs off your face is very uncomfortable.

Keeping your hair color (well, the color it currently is) requires consistency.

And yet—and hear this—you manage to do at least some of these things.

So I want you to keep those things in mind when you start coming up with excuses, and then I want you to punch that excuse in the throat, move past it, get beyond that resistance, and just do it because it matters.

It matters to your business and it matters to your personal satisfaction that you actually follow through with your promise to yourself.

I'm living proof of that.

These days I have the absolute privilege of working with companies all over the world, from Fortune 100 companies to solopreneurs. These people want to be highly successful both in their careers and in their personal lives, not sacrificing one for the other. I get to use my life experiences to encourage others to find their own purpose and pursue it, no matter what life throws at them. I am married to the most incredible man, who is fully supportive of my efforts. My daughter is accomplished and poised for success. She still holds my heart and pushes me to always set an example for her. My son is a delight and so much like me it's scary. He never knew the struggle, and yet his generous, empathetic spirit desires to share all that he has, tangible or in the form of support, with others. My stepdaughter, son-in-law, and granddaughters make me proud every day through their focus on family and their love for our Lord. My extended family, who stuck by me through everything, and my "bonus family" who accepts me and all my crazy ways, along with my fast friends and amazing professional network, round out what I consider an extremely abundant life.

I say none of that to boast. The point is my purpose and my capacity to receive goodness has continuously expanded thanks to the principles I've outlined in this book. It began through raising a child to have all that she deserved in spite of being born to a teenage mother. It evolved into being the best mother and provider for my children I could be, using my career as a tool to create opportunities for their success, and a vision for their future.

Now I get to serve many people who want more out of their own existence, who are divinely discontented to settle for "good enough," and who can use my story to realize they don't have to.

So I invite you right now, for yourself and all the people you impact every day, to embrace your inner Bombshell. I hope this book has made you realize you *can* do it.

Now is your time to declare you are, in fact, a bold, brave, and unwaveringly confident fempreneur.

Notes

Chapter 5

1. KMPG International, *KMPG Women's Leadership Study*, https://womensleadership.kpmg.us/content/dam/kpmg-womens-leadership-golf/womensleadershippressrelease/FINAL%20Womens%20Leadership%20v19.pdf.

2. US Women's Chamber of Commerce, "Women's Businesses Hit with Annual $10 Trillion Opportunity Loss," August 19, 2015, http://uswcc.org/2015/08/womens-businesses-hit-with-10-trillion-opportunity-loss/.

3. United States Census Bureau, "Survey of Business Owners (SBO)," February 23, 2016, https://www.google.com/url?q=https://www.census.gov/library/publications/2012/econ/2012-sbo.html&sa=D&ust=1491612266064000&usg=AFQjCNH45IzOCX6uzUdiwwmcbCuo2JyMUg.

Chapter 6

1. Jim Harter and Amy Adkins, "Employees Want a Lot More from Their Managers," Gallup's *Business Journal*, April 8, 2015, http://www.gallup.com/businessjournal/182321/employees-lot-managers.aspx.

2. David Brown et al., *Culture and Engagement*, Deloitte University Press, February 27, 2015, https://dupress.deloitte.com/dup-us-en/focus/human-capital-trends/2015/employee-engagement-culture-human-capital-trends-2015.html.

3. "Small Business Trends," US Small Business Administration, https://www.sba.gov/managing-business/running-business/energy-efficiency/sustainable-business-practices/small-business-trends.

Chapter 7

1. http://about.americanexpress.com/oc/whoweare/.

Chapter 8

1. Stan Slap, *Under the Hood: Fire Up and Fine-Tune Your Employee Culture* (New York, NY: Portfolio, 2015).

2. https://www.hcareers.com/cjb/loewshotels/.

3. http://www.lq.com/en/navigation/the-bright-side/la-quinta-inn.html.

4. https://c03ccb602f304983f586-6d2431fd9b6a841c5261996358a6ce31.ssl.cf2.rackcdn.com/content/uploads/jwdevelopmentbrochure.pdf.

Chapter 9

1. Jeff Bezos, AZQuotes.com, Wind and Fly LTD, http://www.azquotes.com/quote/614784.

Chapter 10

1. Mark Henricks, "Do You Really Need a Business Plan?" *Entrepreneur*, December 2008, https://www.entrepreneur.com/article/198618.

Chapter 11

1. "Glamour," *Oxford Dictionary* (US), Oxford University Press, https://en.oxforddictionaries.com/definition/us/glamour.

2. Zig Ziglar, *See You at the Top* (Gretna, Louisiana: Pelican Publishing, 2010).

3. Antoine de Saint-Exupéry, Goodreads, http://www.goodreads.com/quotes/87476-a-goal-without-a-plan-is-just-a-wish.

Chapter 12

1. Insights Association, http://www.casro.org/media/Media%20Facts--US%20%28and%20Global%29%20Survey%20Research%20Industry.pdf.

Chapter 14

1. Jim Rohn, Goodreads, http://www.goodreads.com/quotes/1798-you-are-the-average-of-the-five-people-you-spend.

2. John Donne, BrainyQuote.com, https://www.brainyquote.com/quotes/j/johndonne101197.html.

3. Federal Trade Commission, "CAN-SPAM Act: A Compliance Guide for Business," https://www.ftc.gov/tips-advice/business-center/guidance/can-spam-act-compliance-guide-business.

Chapter 15

1. Theodore Roosevelt, BrainyQuote.com, https://www.brainyquote.com/quotes/quotes/t/theodorero100965.html.

Chapter 16

1. Amy Gallo, "The Value of Keeping the Right Customers," *Harvard Business Review*, October 29, 2014, https://hbr.org/2014/10/the-value-of-keeping-the-right-customers.

2. Aristotle, BrainyQuote.com, https://www.brainyquote.com/quotes/quotes/a/aristotle408592.html.

Chapter 17

1. Talya N. Bauer, "Onboarding New Employees: Maximizing Success," SHRM Foundation, https://www.shrm.org/foundation/ourwork/initiatives/resources-from-past-initiatives/Documents/Onboarding%20New%20Employees.pdf.

2. Interactive Services, "New Hire Training: Steps to a Successful Onboarding," http://interactiveservices.com/2014/02/new-hire-training-onboarding/.

3. Suzanne Lucas, "How Much Does It Cost Companies to Lose Employees?", CBSNews.com, http://www.cbsnews.com/news/how-much-does-it-cost-companies-to-lose-employees/.

4. "Independent Contractor (Self-Employed) or Employee?", IRS, https://www.irs.gov/businesses/small-businesses-self-employed/independent-contractor-self-employed-or-employee.

See also: "Hire Your First Employee," US Small Business Administration, https://www.sba.gov/starting-business/hire-retain-employees/hire-your-first-employee.

About the Author

Amber Hurdle understands what it takes to accelerate success. A former teen mom who evolved into a powerhouse businesswoman, Amber has worked with international celebrities and Fortune 500 companies alike. Whether she is empowering female entrepreneurs, teaching them out-of-the-box business strategies, or energizing and educating leadership to boldly next-level their employee engagement, Amber leverages her vast experience throughout multiple entrepreneurial, corporate, and institutional cultures. As the popular host of the *Bombshell Business Podcast,* Amber's straight-shooting "velvet machete" and warm personality never fail to motivate professionals to strategically up their game in business and in life.

Amber holds a degree in Public Relations and Advertising, a dual minor in Marketing and Organizational Communication, and an ACC certification from the International Coaching Federation. She has been featured in national publications such as *Reader's Digest* and *InStyle* magazine, and as an employee engagement expert in the upper division-level textbook *Applied Public Relations: Cases in Stakeholder Management,* 3rd edition, by Kathy Brittain Richardson and Marcie Hinton.

A family woman and friend who loves hard, Amber lives just outside of Nashville with her husband and children. There she enjoys exploring the food scene, cooking with her family and friends, and being a bona fide gym junkie.

Amber offers additional advice and resources on her website, amberhurdle.com, and can be found on Twitter at @amberhurdle.